HISTORY

Rare & Unknown

MIKE WESTBY

DESCHUTES RIVER PRESS
OREGON, U.S.A.

No AI was used in the researching or writing of this book.

Walt Disney's Hyperion Studio business card courtesy of A. Scott Cauger, grandson of A.V. Cauger

ISBN-13: 978-1733598361

20426 - CS

To Elliott and Arlo, our two newest Disney fans.

DISNEY HISTORY
Rare & Unknown

INCLUDES RARE & UNKNOWN STORIES, PHOTOS, AND ITEMS NOT FOUND IN ANY OTHER DISNEY-RELATED BOOKS, ARTICLES OR WEB SITES

As one who enjoys Disney history, specifically the early life of Walt Disney, 1930s Disney merchandise, and the history of Disneyland Resort, I enjoy "pulling the thread" of obscure story elements within these three categories and then delving into the research required to unlock their secrets or uncover a never-before-revealed aspect of the Disney story. This requires untold hours of research, poring through books and papers of all kinds, working with remote libraries and other sources, visiting the theme parks and Disney museums, and interviewing Disney Legends, Disney Imagineers, and other Disney notables.

With *Disney History - Rare & Unknown*, I'm pleased to share what I've uncovered with my fellow Disney enthusiasts. Within these pages, you'll read stories about rare and heretofore unknown facets of Disney history, as well as see rare Disney-related photos, many *of which are being published here for the very first time.*

You'll discover...

- The first-ever-published story about how a 1914 postcard led to my discovery of Ub Iwerks' lost childhood home in Kansas City.

- The *complete* story behind the creation of the very first Hidden Mickey, as told to me by the Imagineer who painted it.

- The first-ever told story about whatever happened to 8 year-old Raymond Sleeper (Now over 70 years old) and the specially built boxcar filled with 10,000 pennies, which Walt awarded him for being the 10 Millionth guest aboard the Disneyland Railroad in August of 1960.

- The never-before-seen ad that Ub Iwerks placed for his "Iwwerks Art Service" business that, for the first time, changes the narrative of Walt and Ub's time after their Iwwerks-Disney business closed up shop in Kansas City.

- The first-ever-told story about Ub Iwerks' father, Eert Ubbe Iwwerks, and his business as an "Out Door Photographer", complete with extremely rare and never-before-seen examples of his photography.

- The fascinating story behind the early history of Disney merchandise, complete with images of rare items.
- The story behind *The Disneyland News*, the now rare 24-page newspaper sold in Disneyland on opening day, July 17, 1955, as told to me by the newspaper's first Editor, Disney Legend Marty Sklar.
- An extremely rare and never-before-seen nearly 100 year-old business card belonging to Walt Disney, from his Walt Disney Studio at 2719 Hyperion.
- The first-ever-told story of the restoration effort behind Walt's beloved Lilly Belle steam engine.
- The never-before-published story of the man who hand carved "The Capitol of Disneyland"...20 years before the park opened.
- The most complete summary published to-date of the work of the Kansas City Slide Co., where Walt and Ub created their very first works of animation.
- A rare 1908 photo of the very cannon in Marceline's E.P. Ripley Park that inspired Walt to put cannons in Disneyland's Town Square.
- Why Disney Legend Emile Kuri chose to buy Main Street, U.S.A.'s gas street lamps 3,000 miles away in Baltimore, MD instead of a location much closer to Disneyland.
- See never-before-seen historic photos of Walt's neighborhood in Kansas City, his newspaper route, Benton Grammar School, Eert Iwwerks' barbershop, the Kansas City Slide Co., and more.

And many, many more stories, all accompanied by an abundance of rarely and never-before-seen photos, graphics, and images not found on the web, with AI, or anywhere else!

TESTIMONIALS

"Holy moly, you have gone way deeper into the weeds of detail for Walt's history than anyone else ever!"

Disney Legend Bob Gurr

"'Disney History - Rare & Unknown' is a gem, a treasure trove of significant behind-the-scene stories of how the granddaddy of all themed attractions came to life, and by whose hands the brilliance of Disneyland's many exceptional authentic attributes found their place within the park's canvas of visual adventure."

John Kuri - Award-winning movie producer, best-selling author, and proud son of Disney Legend Emile Kuri

"Mike Westby's 'Disney History - Rare & Unknown' is an original, groundbreaking, and important work. As an example, with 'He Was The First To Live Walt Disney's Life', Mike has done what no other Disney author has done before: bringing Walt as a young person to life, focusing on what he must've been thinking and feeling as he navigated the significant milestones...and setbacks...in his early life. A fascinating and entertaining read!

A. Scott Cauger - Grandson of A.V. Cauger, Founder of the Kansas City Slide Co.

"For Disney fans who want to know more of the story, they are finally getting it with this masterpiece. The in-depth research done to compile these stories is second to none."

Disney Theme Park Expert Dave Drumheller

FOREWORD
BY DISNEY LEGEND
BOB GURR

Mike Westby's *Disney History - Rare & Unknown* is the latest addition by this renowned Disney Historian to his popular trove of previously published tales of Disney theme park secrets and stories.

This new look at Disney covers a number of interesting stories that visit the Kansas City neighborhoods during Walt's grammar school and paper route life. Readers can get a better sense of what Walt would have seen and experienced on a daily basis. This is important, because this is the very time of life that strongly influences a person's character. I know from personal actual school experience how strongly a caring grammar school teacher can mold a child into a well-rounded adult in later life. Mike furnishes so much written detail about several of Walt's most influential teachers, the reader will gain an even better knowledge of why Walt Disney became a most influential and creative American icon.

Mike has researched this period of Walt's life quite thoroughly, such that you will learn of so many details of his surroundings, even about the most uncomfortable weather that he had to endure while delivering newspapers before dawn in deep snow.

I can attest to what he might have experienced first-hand when I too had to bicycle my paper route in the dark during icy drenching pre-dawn rains before returning home to milk my goats before school. Mike's way of describing Walt's Kansas City days is so full of small details that I could almost feel the joy and discomfort he experienced.

While some of Mike's rare and unknown Disney history pertaining to Disneyland has been explored in prior publications, Mike offers a number of new poignant unpublished experiences, including some I'd never known before. I feel almost embarrassed to not also be aware of them. After all, I was there during the designing and building of Disneyland!

Other little "unknowns" explain how Oscar-winning art director Emile Kuri helped Walt immensely with sourcing all sorts of existing historic artifacts to add to Disneyland, which Emile personally discovered and paid cash for. Both Emile and Frank Millington, Walt's master decorator, worked together to make Disneyland look so perfect and historically accurate. My wife, Louise, along with co-worker Anita Menni, were Emile and Frank's executive secretaries, so I was in on some not-yet-told unknowns with them, too.

I know all of Mike Westby's readers of *Disney History - Rare & Unknown* will learn so much more about Walt Disney's life, and also learn some new details to fill their existing knowledge of Disneyland, especially the secrets of how things got done so fast and who the behind-the-scenes creators were.

Disney Legend Bob Gurr

TABLE OF CONTENTS

Chapter One

1. He Was the First to Live Walt Disney's Life Pg. 15

Chapter Two - Marceline & Kansas City

2. Walt's Inspiration for Disneyland's Cannons Pg. 29
3. Marceline's Midget Autopia Pg. 31
4. Marceline's "Coke Wall" Pg. 34
5. Kansas City, Missouri Pg. 36
6. Walt's Neighborhood Pg. 38
7. Benton Grammar School Pg. 43
8. Walt's Newspaper Route Pg. 49
9. Gertie the Dinosaur & The Wonderland Theatre Pg. 55
10. Animated Cartoons by E.G. Lutz Pg. 57
11. Bert Hudson's Barbershop Pg. 59
12. The Work of the Kansas City Slide Co. Pg. 60
13. Uncovering the Kansas City Slide Co. Pg. 74
14. Walt Disney's Hyperion Studio Business Card Pg. 78
15. Inspiration for Main Street, U.S.A.'s Gas Lamps Pg. 86

Chapter Three - Eert & Ub Iwerks in Kansas City

16. The Discovery of Ub Iwerks' Childhood Home Pg. 93
17. Inside Ub Iwerks' Childhood Home Pg. 100
18. A New Aspect of Ub's Early Childhood Pg. 102
19. Iwwerks Art Service Pg. 105
20. Eert Iwwerks' Barbershop Pg. 106
21. Eert Ubbe Iwwerks - Out Door Photographer Pg. 108

Chapter Four - Disney Merchandise

22. The Early History of Disney Merchandise Pg. 116
23. Kay Kamen's Disney Merchandise Catalogs Pg. 123
24. Mickey & Minnie Save the Day! Pg. 132
25. Mickey & Minnie Save the Day...Again! Pg. 134
26. The $300 "Mystery Man" Pg. 136

Chapter Five - Walt's Love of Trains

27. Walt Disney's Carolwood Pacific Railroad Pg. 142
28. Restoring Walt's Lilly Belle Steam Engine Pg. 149
29. The Restoration of the Lilly Belle Pg. 154
30. Walt Joins the So. California Live Steamers Pg. 160
31. Walt Disney's Old Time Railroad Pg. 166
32. Ward Kimball Interesting Railfans No. 28 Pg. 169

Chapter Six - Walt Disney World

33. The Very First Hidden Mickey Pg. 182
34. Another Original Hidden Mickey Pg. 183
35. Dispelling a Myth - Liberty Square's Liberty Bell Pg. 184
36. A Dreadful Magic Kingdom Murder Mystery Pg. 188
37. The Tumbleweed Cabinet & Casket Co. Pg. 192

Chapter Seven - Disneyland

38. The Capitol of Disneyland Pg. 196
39. The Disneyland News Pg. 201
40. Disneyland - A Fabulous New World Pg. 205
41. A Fair Inspiration for Disneyland Pg. 208
42. A Fair Motivation for Disneyland Pg. 213
43. Disneyland Progresses Pg. 219
44. Orchestrating the Story That is Disneyland Pg. 222
45. Disneyland's Welte Style 4 Orchestrion Pg. 224
46. The Welte Style 4 Orchestrion Before Disneyland Pg. 226
47. Crystal Arts & The Arribas Brothers Pg. 228
48. The Gibson Girl Ice Cream Parlor Pg. 230
49. Fur the Birds, Tuppence a Bag Pg. 232
50. Figaro Makes an "Exit" Pg. 234
51. Emile Kuri Acquires Disneyland's Cannons Pg. 236
52. Why Ship Them All the Way From Baltimore? Pg. 238
53. Main Street, U.S.A.'s Hitching Posts Pg. 241
54. Serendipitous Happenstance Times Two Pg. 243
55. The 10 Millionth Guest of the Disneyland RR Pg. 244
56. A Parting Story Pg. 249

Disney History - Rare & Unknown

As you read this book, you'll find many stories about Walt's early life while growing up in Marceline and Kansas City. However, this is not a biography about Walt, as those books and articles have already been written, many times in fact. Here, I've included biographical information about Walt so as to provide context as you discover rare and unknown stories related to his life and Disney history. While you won't read about such well-known stories as when Walt and Ruth drew on their Marceline home with tar, how Walt worked as a News Butch aboard the Missouri-Pacific, Kansas City Southern, and the Missouri-Kansas-Texas railroads, or how he forged his birth certificate to make his way to France to become a Red Cross Ambulance Corps Driver, you will see and learn about, for the first time, the kind of "animation" he was producing while working at the Kansas City Slide Company, a 1920 ad that changes the narrative about his and Ub's lives post Iwwerks-Disney, and rare and never-before-seen photos of his neighborhood, newspaper route, and the Benton Grammar School in Kansas City, among many other items.

For in-depth biographical information about Walt, I would highly recommend these sources...

- The Walt Disney Family Museum in San Francisco
- The Walt Disney Hometown Museum in Marceline
- *Walt Disney: An American Original* - Bob Thomas
- *Walt Disney - The Triumph of the American Imagination* - Neal Gabler
- *Walt Disney's Missouri - The Roots of a Creative Genius* - Burnes, Butler, & Viets
- *Walt Before Mickey - Disney's Early Years, 1919 - 1928* - Timothy S. Susanin

Chapter One

He Was The First to Live Walt Disney's Life

HE WAS THE FIRST TO LIVE WALT DISNEY'S LIFE

As we read about and study Walt Disney's life, it's interesting to consider that we do so through the crystal clear yet distorted lens of absolute certainty, already knowing that with every decision Walt made and every step that he took, be it resulting in success or failure at the time, they would all ultimately lead him to tremendous success where hundreds of millions of people around the world would know not only his name, but also the animated characters he worked so diligently to create.

Walt as a Red Cross Ambulance Corps driver while in France - 1919. (Used with Permission - Pg. 25)

For Walt, however, he was not that fortunate. Being the first person to "experience" Walt Disney's life while living its narrative, he had none of the casual certainty that we enjoy while looking back at his life more than 100 years later.

Arriving back home from France in the fall of 1919, he was no doubt filled with confidence after his life-changing overseas tour as an ambulance driver at the end of WWI. With this confidence, as well as his increasing skills as an artist, he approached the Kansas City Star, one of three major Kansas City newspapers, for a job as a cartoonist. At the time, daily newspapers were some of the most prestigious employers around. Radio was still in its infancy, and there was no such thing as television yet, so print was king, be it in magazines, posters, brochures, or newspapers, and of all of those, the Kansas City Star represented one of the most powerful voices in the community, reaching over *215,000* readers twice every day. Walt was shooting for the top, so it must have rattled him considerably when he was rejected by the newspaper. Of course, we read this news as a small footnote to his story, since we're already aware of the next step he took on his path to success, but at the time, he probably felt a great deal of doubt, uncertainty, and worry, because to him his future was unknown. All he did know for sure was that the stock market was dropping, the American economy was slowing now that the war was over, and soldiers by the tens of thousands were arriving back home from Europe and competing for a dwindling number of jobs...and he was one of them

Pesmen-Rubin Commercial Art Studio

Needing work, Walt approached the Pesmen-Rubin Commercial Art Studio for a job, where he took an apprenticeship helping with the coming Christmas season rush. Relieved to be working, he was perhaps concerned that he'd once again find himself unemployed soon after the holidays were over, when business would slow again...and then what would he do? Today, we read about this stage in Walt's life and realize that, unbeknownst to him, it would be at this Pesmen-Rubin job that he'd meet a fellow 19 year-old, Ub Iwwerks, forming a friendship that would ultimately allow him to create a worldwide phenomenon only eight years later...Mickey Mouse. However, Mickey hadn't even crossed Walt's mind yet. For him, all *he* knew was that this job was going to end, and soon.

Iwwerks-Disney Commercial Artists

The answer to that question came in the form of his new endeavor, Iwwerks-Disney Commercial Artists, which he formed with Ub after being laid off from his Pesmen-Rubin job in January of 1920. Here, he and Ub would create advertisements and illustrations for local businesses. Unfortunately, finding paying clients for their fledgling startup was difficult, and within only a short time Walt was beginning to feel the all too familiar troubling sense of failure once again...only a short while after he had been laid off from his Pesmen-Rubin job and only a few months since he had returned from France. It was about this time when he saw a job listing posted by the Kansas City Slide Company for an artist position, one which would involve drawing advertising slides for display with silent movies. Discussing the opportunity with Ub, they both agreed Walt should apply for the job. He did, and at the end of January he was hired.

Kansas City Slide Company

It's important to understand the context of Walt's new position. At the time, silent movies were extremely popular all across the country, since they were the only form of quality entertainment accessible to the general public. Radio, while invented in 1895, was not widely available yet, and televisions wouldn't begin to appear in America's living rooms for another 30 years. Vaudeville acts on stage were quickly giving way to motion pictures as silent film stars like Charlie Chaplin, Buster Keaton, Douglas Fairbanks, and Mary Pickford ushered in an exciting new era in story-telling and entertainment. Large opulent movie houses filled with crowds in grand formal settings every weekend, while smaller theaters popped up in rural towns all across America. Everyone wanted to see the new silent movies, as this was the future, and the future had arrived!

As the silent movies and movie houses prospered, so did the busy Kansas City Slide Company. Businesses and movie houses could contract to have all manner of slides produced for advertisements or announcements to be shown on the big screen, each costing anywhere from 33 cents to $1.50.

Kansas City Slide Co.
Walt Disney is seated in the back left hand corner desk

As Walt settled into his desk on his first day of work, I wonder what he was feeling? Peering into the future, did he optimistically sense this new potential for success, or did he instead see the darkening clouds of failure once again, since his original plan had called for him to be working at one of the two prestigious Kansas City newspapers by this time. Did he worry that if this job didn't work out he may have to give up his dreams of having an artistic career and instead get a job distributing newspapers again, like his father? Today, it's almost comical for us to think about, from our viewpoint, how his life was soon about to set off on a grand or even "magical" course, but to him, he had no sense of the future yet, only a clear understanding of the present, which was proving to be very difficult and, perhaps most troubling for him, once again uncertain.

While the future was unknown, Walt was no doubt taking stock. Movie houses were filled with moviegoers, so he knew where to find an audience that was eager to be entertained. In addition, he knew of the science and process of animation, and while it was still in its infancy, it had clearly been proven to work. Winsor McCay had invented the mutoscope twenty five

years prior, in 1895, providing penny arcades across the country with a popular new form of entertainment which, in a manner very similar to animation, employed the technique of flipping 800 to 900 photos on a circular reel in rapid succession past a small viewer, thus giving a paying customer the sense of fluid movement for a story lasting about one minute. 19 Years later, in 1914, Mr. McCay produced *Gertie the Dinosaur*, an innovative silent cartoon considered by many to be the very first cartoon ever produced. It was also about this time that Walt began carefully studying two books; *Animated Cartoons: How They Are Made, Their Origin and Development* by E.G. Lutz, and *Animals in Motion* by Eadweard Muybridge, both of which taught Walt not only how to *draw* cartoons, but how to *create* the animated end product, as well. Now, while the nascent world of animation was taking shape, Walt was immersed on a daily basis in a job that gave him first hand exposure to the actual art, craft, and science of making animated films, even though the films they produced in the now renamed Kansas City Film Ad Service were nothing more than simple silent advertisements using rudimentary stop-motion animation involving physical cutout characters, a technique far different from the drawings Walt and Ub would ultimately employ.

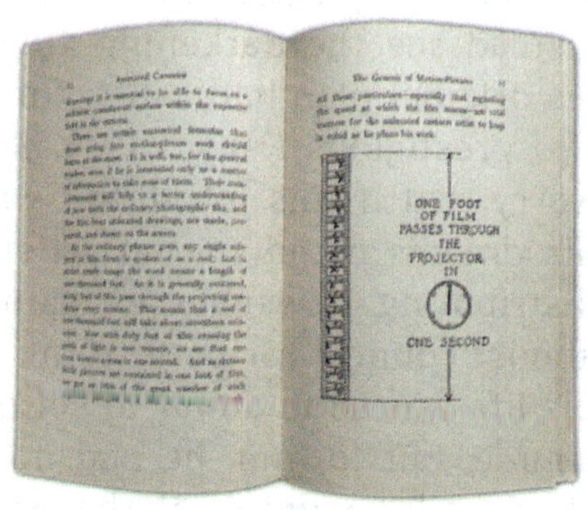
ONE FOOT
OF FILM
PASSES THROUGH
THE
PROJECTOR
IN
ONE SECOND

Seeing a waiting audience, understanding the craft and science of animation, and now having first-hand experience in producing animated films, Walt must have been filled with inspiration. Borrowing a camera from the shop, he began drawing and filming a short series of animated films he called *Local Happenings*, which focused on topics of local interest, such as social issues, reported crimes, and ladies fashion. Walt showed these to his boss, A.V. Cauger, who, impressed by his work, suggested he show them to Frank Newman, owner of the newly built $2,000,000 Newman Theatre. Designed in a grand and opulent style to host 2,000 patrons per showing, and proclaimed to be "The Supreme Achievement in Motion Picture Presentation", it was the most expensive theatre ever built in Kansas City at the time, and a showing here of Walt's work would surely be a feather in his cap.

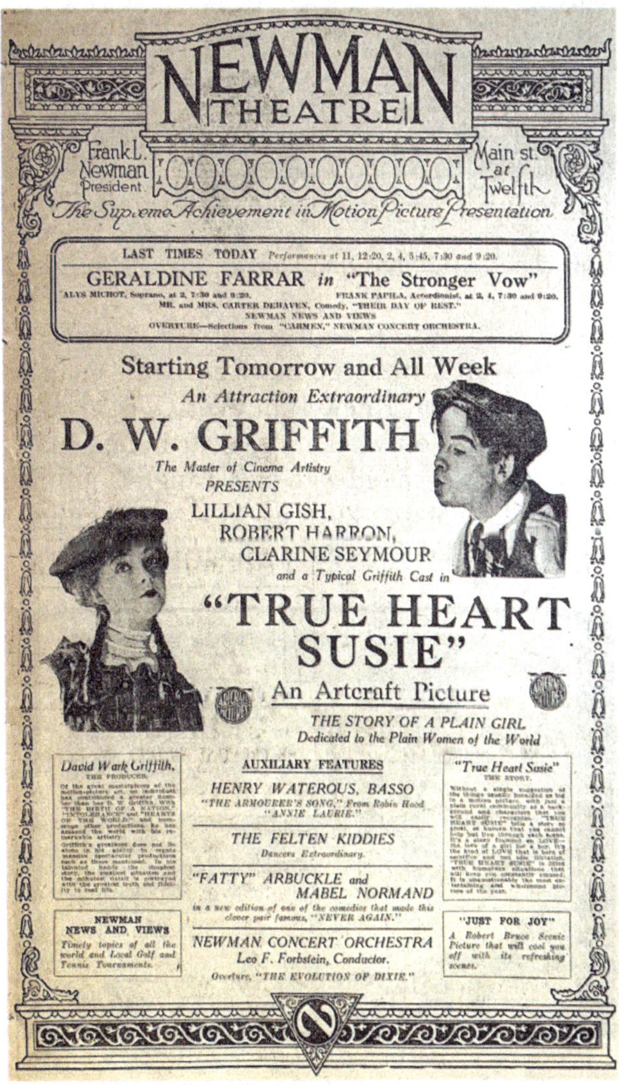

June 29, 1919 ad for the Newman Theatre
Author's Collection

Newman Theatre Auditorium - Kansas City, MO – Circa 1919

Impressed with Walt's animation, Mr. Newman not only agreed to show Walt's films at the Newman Theatre, but also contracted with him for a new film every week. Working late into the evenings and on weekends, Walt honed his animation skills creating what he called Newman Laugh-O-grams, the first of which debuted on March 20th of 1921, a little over one year after Walt started at the Kansas City Slide Company.

Newman Laugh-O-grams Image
Bearing a resemblance to Walt's upcoming business card

Now, for the first time, Walt was experiencing success on a larger scale. His animated films, while short and topical, weren't playing at a small rural theatre holding perhaps a couple hundred people, but instead were being seen by an audience of up to 2,000 people multiple times a day at Kansas City's grandest theatre. He continued to produce the Newman Laugh-O-grams for the next several months before deciding to set out once again on his own, and in May of 1922 he incorporated his new business, Laugh-O-grams Films, Inc.

Laugh-O-grams Films, Inc.

Emboldened, Walt, Ub, and a staff of five other young animators, along with four supporting staff, set out to make Laugh-O-grams a success, but while they all worked diligently to produce a series of films, their clients' payments for those films were not arriving in a timely manner, and Walt soon found himself without the funds to pay his staff.

Unable to meet payroll, his employees began to leave one by one, including Ub, who returned to work for Kansas City Film Ad Service. To help preserve what few funds were left, Walt moved from his apartment to the Laugh-O-grams studio, where he would now sleep and work, at night watching and studying the small mice that would emerge from the shadows to search for any food they could find. One in particular became comfortable with Walt and would frequently pay him a visit, resting on his desk while Walt drew. While the move to his studio was a bold step, it still didn't assuage his fears of failure. Taking stock, he had few funds, his staff had left, he had no long-term projects in development, and the one company he was counting on to provide any income at all, Pictorial Clubs, had gone bankrupt. On top of this, he was relying upon the generosity of the owners of the Forest Inn Café for free meals, he was shaving in a public restroom, and he had to travel to the busy Union Station to use the public baths for bathing.

The McConahy Building at E. 31st and Forest Ave.
Walt's Laugh-O-grams office was located on the second floor, behind the last three sets of double windows at the far right

Years later, he would admit that during this time he felt "crushed and heartbroken." Referencing the local train station, he said...

> *"I used to go down and stand there with tears in my eyes and look at the trains going out...I was all alone. I was very lonesome."*

All the while, Walt's brother, Roy, had been out in California recovering from a bout of tuberculosis. Walt had been keeping Roy apprised of his ongoing trials, and Roy responded that it was time for Walt to leave Kansas City and join him out west. "*Kid, I think you should get out of there. I don't think you can do any more for it.*" Realizing his brother was right, Walt packed his clothes into a cardboard suitcase, along with a copy of his most recent project, *Alice's Wonderland*, and headed west with only $40 in his pocket and a great deal of uncertainty...and optimism...for a better future. True to form, he paid for and traveled with a first class ticket.

Walt Disney wartime photo courtesy of The Walt Disney Family Museum

Chapter Two

Marceline & Kansas City, MO

MARCELINE, MO

Shortly after Walt was born in Chicago on December 5, 1901, his father, Elias, became concerned that the bustling city was becoming less and less of a proper place to raise a family. In talking with his brother, Robert, Elias was encouraged to move his family to the small town of Marceline, Missouri and try his hand at farming. His brother knew just the place for them to settle, a 45-acre spread with a simple farmhouse, a barn, and some livestock.

"I went with my family to live in Marceline when I was four years old. I clearly remember the day we arrived there on the train. A Mr. Coffman met us in his wagon and we rode out to our house in the country just outside the city limits. I believe it was called the Crane Farm. My first impression of it was that it had a beautiful front yard." - Walt Disney

Walt had no idea at the time, but this simple move would have a profound impact upon not just himself as a young boy, but his future as well, for here he was quickly immersed in a world of wide open fields, shady groves, a flowing stream, a friendly old barn, and a collection of different farm animals, each with their own personalities. It was this world that would give birth to his creativity and forge happy memories that would last his lifetime.

"To tell the truth, more things of importance happened to me in Marceline than have happened to me since or are likely to in the future." - Walt Disney

Growing on the farm was a majestic Cottonwood tree. Rising from a broad trunk, it towered into the sun, providing Walt with a shady spot next to a small stream where he would draw the different farm animals and dream of the adventures they'd experience. It was this spot, under his "Dreaming Tree", that Walt would credit as being the birthplace of his creativity.

Walt's Inspiration for Disneyland's Cannons

It was in Marceline that Walt would experience for the very first time many things that would inspire him later in his life. Living on the family's farm, he studied and drew the barnyard animals that would play such prominent roles in his early animated cartoons and films. Massive steam trains rolling by on the edge of town with their whistles blowing would kindle his life-long love of trains, and the small town's quaint main street would provide one of the primary inspirations for the design of Disneyland's Town Square and Main Street, U.S.A.

In the heart of Marceline, on Kansas Avenue, was E.P. Ripley Park. No doubt Walt occasionally ventured here from the family farm to spend the afternoon playing with his friends, or perhaps rode to the park in a horse and buggy with his father, when Elias would play his fiddle on warm summer evenings in the park's white gazebo, while nearby a fountain bubbled from its ornate column topped with a cherub, and children played in the cool shaded grass.

Years later, when Walt was designing Disneyland's Town Square, he wanted to include story elements that reminded him of small towns in America's mid-west. These elements included welcoming park benches, a majestic flag pole, chuffing steam trains departing for points beyond, and two military cannons, as many small mid-west towns had a cannon in their city park as a tribute to the town's veterans.

One of the two cannons in Disneyland's Town Square

At the beginning of this article is an extremely rare postcard featuring the actual Civil War cannon that used to be on display in Marceline's E.P. Ripley Park during the years when Walt lived there as a boy, and it is likely that *this is the very cannon that provided Walt with the inspiration to include the two cannons found in Disneyland's town square today.* Taken in 1908, the photo shows the exact same view of the cannon that Walt would have seen when he played in the park as a young boy, during the years of 1905 to 1911. In the background of the postcard image is the building housing the 1906 Allen Hotel, which still stands today, awaiting its return to its former glory. Unfortunately, the cannon no longer exists, as it was melted down for scrap, likely during World War II.

1908 Cannon postcard - Author's Collection

Marceline's Midget Autopia

Original Disneyland Midget Autopia Car
As displayed in the Walt Disney Hometown Museum

Disneyland's Autopia has been very popular with young drivers since opening day in 1955, and even today, no matter what time you visit the attraction, you'll find it bustling with activity. Day or night, the air is filled with the sound of accelerating engines, squealing hot brakes, clanking bumpers, and shouts of excitement as young guests eagerly take the wheel of a stylish sports car and hit the open road. Shortly after Disneyland opened, it became apparent that this attraction was a big hit and everyone wanted to ride it, not only those who slid behind the wheel, but also those guests who were left on the side of the road wishing they, too, were tall enough to reach the gas pedal. To accommodate these younger guests, Walt soon created Junior Autopia, and on May 13, 1956, its cars took to a new track, separate from the original Autopia and complete with "booster blocks", which allowed younger drivers to reach the gas pedal just as their taller brothers and sisters could on the original Autopia.

Very quickly, the new Junior Autopia also proved to be a big hit. However, it soon became apparent that yet another Autopia was needed, one for even smaller guests, perhaps as young as 4 years of age, and on April 23, 1957, Disneyland welcomed its third Autopia attraction, Midget Autopia.

Featuring the smallest of the three Autopia tracks, Midget Autopia took its young yet adventurous guests on a casual drive through the "countryside" instead of California's fast-paced Freeways. Riding in cars built specifically for their smaller stature, complete with a stylish chrome Hood Rocket from the popular 1957 Chevy, the young drivers made their way along a short and winding route past landscaped hillsides before "crashing" through the doors of a small yellow barn. Unlike the Autopia and Junior Autopia cars, these smaller cars were the domain of only these youngest of children, as they were too small for older kids and adults to fit into. Two steering wheels allowed both occupants to "drive", though the cars kept to the center of the road with the help of a center bus bar, which not only prevented any accidents from occurring, but also governed the acceleration, speed, and braking of the vehicles, much to the delight of waiting parents. Unfortunately, the days of Midget Autopia were numbered, however.

Walt and his Imagineers were invited to design and build a number of attractions for the 1964 / 1965 New York World's Fair, and one of these was the now iconic "it's a small world". Walt had planned on moving this attraction to Disneyland after the World's Fair finished, so in April of 1966 he closed Midget Autopia to make room for "it's a small world" and its coming debut on May 28, 1966.

With the Midget Autopia attraction now without a home, Walt, along with his brother Roy, decided to donate its 10 small cars and track components to his childhood hometown, Marceline, Missouri.

Midget Autopia in Marceline, Missouri
Photo courtesy of the Walt Disney Hometown Museum

Only a few short months after it closed at Disneyland, Midget Autopia traversed a new track in Marceline's Walt Disney Municipal Park, opening there on July 4, 1966. Just as with Disneyland, the new attraction was a big hit with the young drivers of Marceline. Unfortunately, where Disneyland had the manpower, tools and expertise to maintain such an attraction, the small town of Marceline did not, and the attraction slowly fell into a state of disrepair over time. Eleven years after its arrival, the town was forced to cease its operation, and the components of Midget Autopia were tucked away into a barn to be saved for another day. That day arrived on May 14th of 2022 when Marceline dedicated its newly restored Midget Autopia attraction, and today new electric cars patterned after the original models can be found plying a winding track right next door to the Walt Disney Hometown Museum, complete with a bright yellow shed that mirrors the original found in Disneyland.

MARCELINE'S "COKE WALL"

Admittedly, the following story may not qualify as rare and unknown, but the tale is a good one that relates to Walt and his time in Marceline. It also ties in nicely with another story you'll find on Page 192.

If you travel to Marceline, you'll no doubt come across the large "Coke Wall". As shared with me by the Walt Disney Hometown Museum during their gracious tour of the town, Walt at one point had made mention of the large Coca-Cola mural he used to see as a boy in Marceline whenever he went into town. However, it was pointed out to Walt that he must be mistaken, as nobody knew of a Coca-Cola mural having ever existed in Marceline. Despite the naysayers, Walt steadfastly insisted it was there. On April 8, 2002, an apartment building on the corner of W. Ritchie Ave. and N. Kansas Ave. burned, and when the debris was cleared, much to everyone's surprise there appeared on the exterior wall of the building next door...a large Coca-Cola mural! Estimated to have been painted over an old Owl Cigar mural in 1906, when Walt and his family lived in Marceline, the Coca-Cola mural was covered up by the apartment building, which was built in front of it in 1919.

Pleased to have "added" a large new historical story element to Marceline, the City reached out to the Coca-Cola Company to make them aware of their discovery. In turn, the Coca-Cola Company sent a team of artists to repaint the mural, and in December of 2015 they presented the restored brightly painted facade as a gift to the Walt Disney Company, and ultimately Marceline, as a tribute to their 60 year partnership.

KANSAS CITY, MO

Walt and his family moved to Kansas City from Marceline in 1911, when Walt was only 9 years old, and while the years spent in Marceline reflected the slower pace of rural farm life, his Kansas City years moved with a quicker cadence, a tempo that played an important role in shaping his work ethic, developing his artistic abilities, and, after a series of setbacks, launching him toward his future success.

In this chapter, you'll find many Disney-related stories tied to Walt Disney's and Ub Iwerks' time in Kansas City. While nearly every book I've read leaves it to the reader's imagination to picture Walt's neighborhood, his newspaper route, where Ub lived, and even James M. Cottingham, who was Walt's principal at Benton Grammar School, I set out to find actual photos of these Disney history elements, as well as uncover and present never-before-published information. Here, you'll read about my solving of a perplexing mystery that led to the discovery of Ub Iwerks' lost childhood home, discover never-before-published photos and information about Walt's time at the Kansas City Slide Co., see the first-ever published photo of Eert Iwwerks' barbershop, learn of the inspiration for the gas street lamps Walt placed on Disneyland's Main Street, U.S.A., and even see photos that give you an understanding of the kind of homes Walt delivered newspapers to while on his daily newspaper route.

The following bullet points summarize key moments during Walt's time in Kansas City, thus providing context for the articles that follow...

- The Disney's first home in Kansas City was at 2706 E. 31st Street. Located just off busy 31st and with neighboring houses almost within reach on each side, it was a big change from Marceline's open spaces and quiet rural farm life for young Walt.

- Shortly after they arrived, Walt's father, Elias, put Walt and his brother, Roy, to work delivering newspapers in a 24 block area immediately north of their home, known as the Santa Fe neighborhood, and this was a job that Walt would continue to perform nearly every day, rain or shine, until he was 16 years old.

- In 1914, Walt and his family moved three blocks east to a home at 3028 Bellefontaine Ave., just north of E. 31st Street.

- Walt began attending Benton Grammar School at age 9, and he continued there until age 17, when his family moved back to Chicago. Benton Grammar School was conveniently located a little over two blocks from his home at 2706 E. 31st Street, and three blocks from 3028 Bellefontaine Ave.

- In 1917, Walt reunited with his family in Chicago, where his father, as an investor, accepted a role with the O-Zell Jelly Company. Walt worked there briefly as a bottle washer, but in the fall of 1918, he altered the year of his birth on his birth certificate and enlisted in the Red Cross Ambulance Corps, shipping off to France just as WWI was officially ending, though the situation there was still tumultuous and at times dangerous. Ten months later, he returned home, heading back to Kansas City to stay in the house at 3028 Bellefontaine, which was now occupied by his brother, Herbert.

- Filled with confidence after returning home from overseas, Walt attempted to begin a career as an illustrator and animator, but after repeated failed attempts at finding long-term employment or starting his own business, he took his brother Roy's advice to join him in Los Angeles, packed his suitcase, and in August of 1923 boarded a train and headed west to his unknown future. His friend, Ub Iwerks, would soon follow at Walt's request.

WALT'S NEIGHBORHOOD

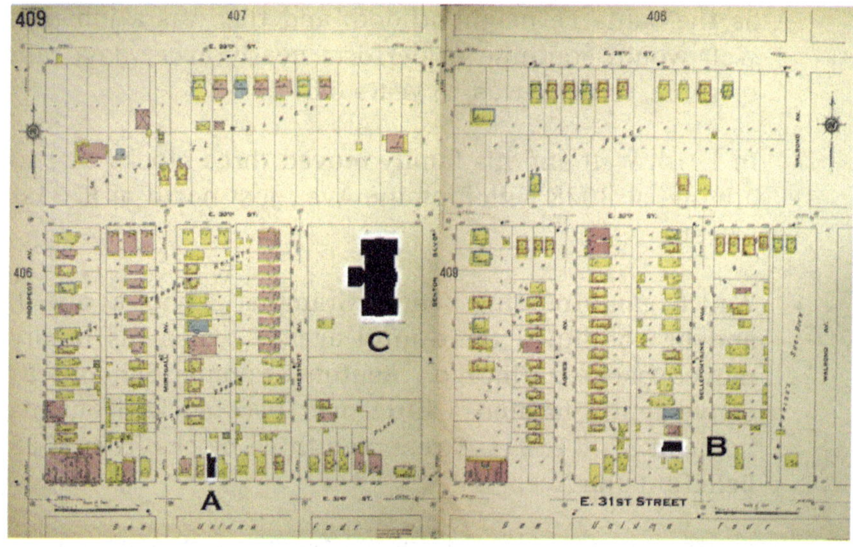

1909 Plat Map - Two years before the Disney family arrived in 1911
A - 2706 E. 31st Street
B - 3028 Bellefontaine Ave.
C - Benton Grammar School
Laugh-O-gram Studios was located on E. 31st Street, approximately 20 blocks west of Walt's Bellefontaine Ave. home

Map Courtesy of Missouri Valley Special Collections - Kansas City Public Library

Walt lived in two different homes in Kansas City during three different periods. In 1911, at the age of 9, he and his family moved from Marceline, Missouri to a home at 2706 E. 31st Street, (A) and sometime in 1914, reportedly so as to get off of busy 31st, the Disneys moved to 3028 Bellefontaine Ave., (B) only a few blocks to the east. After graduating from Benton Grammar School, Walt would follow his parents and sister to Chicago in 1917, before moving back to the Bellefontaine Ave. address again after returning home from France in 1919.

As you picture Walt's neighborhood, you may have a bit of a vague sense of how it looked in the early 1900s, even drawing upon your own neighborhood in an attempt to reach back in time to form an image in your mind. Mentally, you fill in the style of homes that lined the boulevards, the honking traffic made up of "modern" Model Ts, perhaps a few horse-drawn delivery wagons passing by, and maybe a fleeting sense of the busy streets, the neighborhood parks, the nearby businesses, and other elements that formed the backdrop to Walt's daily life.

The Disney Home at 3028 Bellefontaine Ave.
Photo Courtesy of the National Archives

Like most neighborhoods across the country that are bisected by a busy thoroughfare, the "identity" of Walt's neighborhood was connected to E. 31st Street. Running east to west, it was lined with tightly packed homes and a collection of single to three-story businesses and apartment buildings, all of which created a stark contrast to rural Marceline's slower-paced main street, Kansas Avenue. His home at 2706 E. 31st Street (A) looked directly out onto the road, much to his mother's dismay, while his later home on Bellefontaine Ave. (B) was situated as the second home north of E. 31st Street.

A horse drawn carriage passes Benton Grammar School during the period in which Walt attended as a young boy
Author's Collection

As a young boy, when Walt walked E. 31st Street, perhaps on his way to Benton Grammar School or the bakery just a few doors down from his home, he experienced first-hand the short period in time when horse-drawn carriages and delivery wagons were giving way to the new gasoline powered automobiles and trucks of the era, especially the shiny new Model T. In fact, I'm guessing it must have been a bit of a novelty for Walt to see one coming his way in 1911, announcing the future's arrival with its distinct "Ahhoooga!" sounding horn.

Benton Grammar School was located at E. 30th Street and Benton Blvd., (C) a little over one block east and one block north of his home at 2706 E. 31st Street, and two blocks west and one block north of his home on Bellefontaine. On his walks to school, he'd walk a couple of blocks over to Benton Blvd., where he'd then turn north at the corner and continue a short distance to the Benton Grammar School on the left at the end of the block.

While the home on Bellefontaine Ave. and the Benton Grammar School still exist today, the home at 2706 E. 31st Street has been demolished and lost to time.

Benton Blvd. looking north from E. 31st Street - Circa 1910
This is similar to how Benton Blvd. looked when Walt lived here
Author's Collection

Benton Blvd. was more residential and perhaps a bit more upper class than E. 31st Street, for here was a wide boulevard stretching north to south, its curbs on each side lined with uniform trees and elegant gas street lamps set into wide manicured grass borders. Sidewalks ran the length of each block, and the large stately homes perched on a berm above street level conveyed a sense of affluence to passersby.

E. 31st Street also formed the southern border of the square 24 block area that encompassed Walt and Roy's newspaper route, known as the Santa Fe neighborhood. Benton Blvd. bisected the neighborhood, and the houses found along their routes varied from impressive larger homes to smaller row houses and apartment buildings, all of varied designs, with many reflecting design elements of the new Craftsman style.

If the Disney family needed a product or service, they typically didn't need to travel far to get it, as their neighborhood was filled with a variety of small businesses scattered among its streets. Within walking distance were four barbershops, including Bert Hudson's, a confectionery, a couple of theatres, a dentist, a jeweler, a plumber and a market. Charlie Tong's Laundry would clean your shirts, as would Benton Cleaner and Tailors. The Perfect Shoe Repair Shop could pull the nail out of the toe of a boot, while J.H. Anderson Hardware could replace it. Zinn's Drug Store at 31st and Prospect offered a variety of goods, and the Central Beauty Shoppe offered ladies in the neighborhood permanent waves and manicures. And when someone needed ice for their refrigerator or coal for a fire, then all they had to do was ring the operator and ask her to place a call to E. M. Rounds at "Linwood 1296". (That's an old-fashioned phone number.)

Walt's neighborhood was like most others in Kansas City, in that it conveyed not only a sense of pride and community, but also a sense of energy. It was busy, and unknown to Walt at the time, it was filled with elements that would leave a number of strong impressions on him that would last his lifetime, as well as greatly affect the course of his life.

The old-fashioned phone seen here is the actual phone found today in Tiana's Bayou General Store in the Magic Kingdom.

BENTON GRAMMAR SCHOOL

Benton Grammar School - Circa 1920s
From the 1925 Bentonian Yearbook
Note the gas street lamp on the corner
Author's Collection

On September 5, 1911, only a few months after arriving in Kansas City, Walt began attending the nearby Benton Grammar School, a massive three story brick building with stone accents located on the stately tree-lined Benton Boulevard. The school was an impressive structure for its time, and one well-suited for the affluence of the neighborhood. Inside, gas lamps illuminated the hallways leading to a dozen different classrooms, while outside, tall gas street lamps dotted the sidewalks and streets being traversed by pedestrians and horse drawn buggies and wagons.

As a result of rising in the early morning darkness every day to deliver his newspapers, as well as leaving school early every afternoon to begin his 4:00 p.m. route, Walt struggled here as a student, and he was the first to admit that his grades reflected this. At times, however, he excelled. In the fifth grade, while showing a penchant for performing, he donned an Abraham Lincoln costume, complete with his father's frock coat and a stovepipe hat made of cardboard, and recited the Gettysburg Address to his class. His act was so entertaining that his teacher alerted the principal, James M. Cottingham, who in turn enthusiastically took Walt to every classroom in the school so he could repeat his performance, no doubt much to Walt's delight. Soon, Walt, along with his friend Walt Pfeiffer, were entering talent contests at the nearby Agnes Theatre, performing as different characters, including the popular Charlie Chaplin and his nemesis, The Count.

Photo of Principal J. M. Cottingham
1925 Bentonian Yearbook

"I remember how Principal Cottingham would break in on any classes if he had a new story and all work would cease until he had had his fun. He had his faults, but I think of him as a swell fellow."

- Walt Disney

Two extremely rare 1925 & 1931 copies of The Bentonian yearbook
Mike Westby and David Lesjak collections

While Walt wasn't the best student, he was well liked by his teachers and fellow students, especially his 7th grade teacher, Miss Daisy Beck, whom he credited with encouraging and promoting his love of drawing, acting, and storytelling, even while struggling with his grades.

> *"Miss Beck...saw what she regarded as potential talents in other kids, too, and did everything she could to bring them out. The point is, she tried to understand all of us as individuals. But she never favored or pampered any of us. She managed somehow to promote our personal inclinations without neglecting the formal grade requirements."*
>
> *"She knew that the good students, the apt ones, who got their lessons easily would get along well without much urging or coaching. It was the laggards, like myself, who most needed encouragement. So with great patience and understanding, and incredible faith, she lavished her teaching genius upon the least promising of her charges."* - Walt Disney

Walt graduated in the spring of 1917, and approximately 13 years later, when Mickey Mouse was beginning to take the world by storm, Principal Cottingham wrote to him and asked if he would reply with a post-graduation update. Walt gladly responded with a letter in which he shared his thoughts about the years he spent at Benton and what they meant to him. In addition, he included a special drawing of Mickey Mouse. In turn, Principal Cottingham reprinted the letter in its entirety within the 1931 Bentonian yearbook, along with the Mickey Mouse drawing, which was featured on the back cover. Disney historian and author David Lesjak owns one of only two known examples of this yearbook. What follows is a portion of Walt's February 18, 1931 letter to Principal Cottingham...

"I have often thought of you and my former teachers at Benton and have always had a feeling that I should enjoy a little visit with you on one of my trips to New York.

When I was in school, Benton had a record of winning the K.C.A.C. meet six years in succession. I have often wondered what sort of record the school has held since that time. I was graduated from Benton in June of 1917 and spent my last year under Miss Beck. I have often wondered about Miss Beck, and if she is still teaching in Kansas City.

My high school career was very short. After I was graduated I worked during the summer as a News Butch on the railroad, and the following fall moved to Chicago. I spent my freshman year there. Following that I joined the Red Cross as an ambulance driver and went to France. I returned from France in the fall of 1919.

I went to Kansas City, and started to work for the Grey Advertising Company as an Apprentice Artist. I left that company to work for the Film Service Company of Kansas City, and it was there that I learned the work that I am still engaged in. While I was working with the Film Service Company I made a short weekly film for Frank Newman, and this led to the establishing of a Studio of my own. I made cartoon versions of fairy tales, but this venture was not successful.

I moved to California in 1923 and started in business with my brother Roy. Since that time we have built our business up to what it is today, and at the present time we have a Studio employing about seventy-five persons, both artists and technicians.

I thank you for your interest, and extend to you my best personal regards.

My best personal regards to you, Walt Disney"

Miss Daisy Beck

In 1942, no doubt after seeing the great success of such films as Snow White and the Seven Dwarfs, Fantasia, Pinocchio, and of course the worldwide fame of Mickey Mouse, Walt's favorite teacher, Daisy Beck, extended an invitation for him to return to Kansas City and the Benton Grammar School for a reunion. Walt gladly accepted, returning, along with Clarence Nash, the voice of Donald Duck, to share tales of his continuing success and world travels, as well as to share two of his cartoons with an estimated 800 students, teachers, and parents. That evening, he enjoyed a dinner hosted by Miss Beck in a private residence. Though a poor student, Walt was now recognized as an honored graduate of the Benton Grammar School.

My thanks to David Lesjak for his generous contributions to this article, including the images from his rare 1931 issue of The Bentonian.

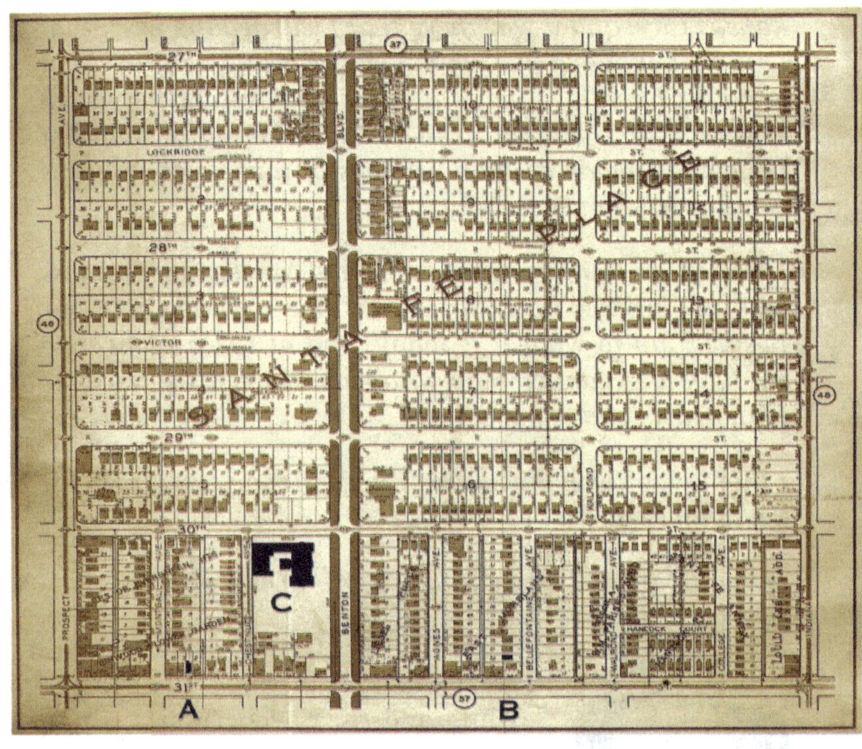

1925 Plat Map of Walt's Entire Newspaper Route

A - 2706 E. 31st Street
B - 3028 Bellefontaine Ave.
C - Benton Grammar School

Map Courtesy of Missouri Valley Special Collections - Kansas City Public Library

WALT'S NEWSPAPER ROUTE

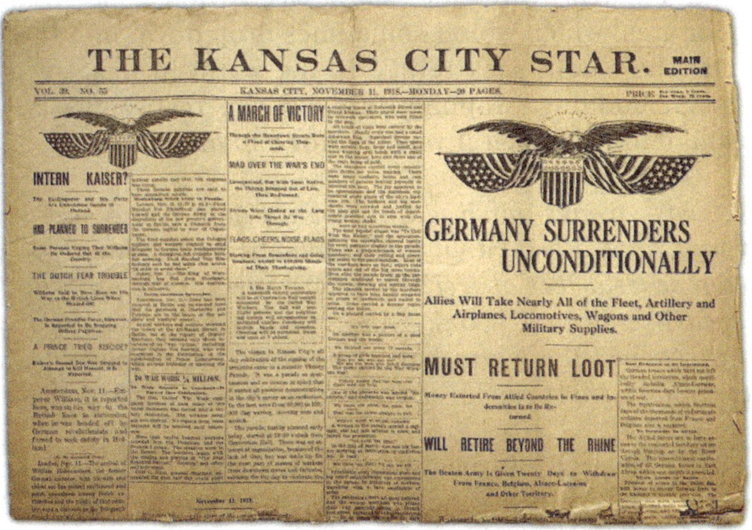

THE KANSAS CITY STAR. MAIN EDITION

INTERN KAISER?

HAD PLANNED TO SURRENDER

THE DUTCH FEAR TROUBLE

A PRINCE TRIED SUICIDE?

A MARCH OF VICTORY

MAD OVER THE WAR'S END

FLAGS, CHEERS, NOISE, FLAGS

GERMANY SURRENDERS UNCONDITIONALLY

Allies Will Take Nearly All of the Fleet, Artillery and Airplanes, Locomotives, Wagons and Other Military Supplies.

MUST RETURN LOOT

WILL RETIRE BEYOND THE RHINE

Rare Kansas City Star Newspaper from November 11, 1918
Author's Collection

"When I was nine, my brother Roy and I were already businessmen. We had a newspaper route...delivering papers in a residence area every morning and evening of the year, rain, shine, or snow. We got up at 3:30 a.m., worked until the school bell rang and did the same thing again from four o'clock in the afternoon until supper time."

- Walt Disney

From age 9 until he was 15, Walt and his brother, Roy, delivered newspapers for their father's newspaper route. His day would begin at 3:30 a.m., when he would venture out into the cold darkness to pick up his heavy allotment of the Kansas City Times. Working through the dawn, he would struggle with the weight of the newspapers as he hustled along his route, making sure he was home in time to have some breakfast, grab a quick nap if he was lucky, and then head off to school, where he would oftentimes struggle to stay awake and pay attention. Leaving school early every day, he would repeat the process with his afternoon deliveries of the Kansas City Star before heading home. Winters were especially difficult, as Walt would struggle to deal with the snow, ice, wind, and freezing temperatures, which would sometimes drop down into the 20s. At times, he would seek refuge in the warm lit hallway of an apartment building, stopping to sit down, rest, and ward off the chill, telling himself it was just for a moment...

It was always pitch dark when I left home on winter mornings, and often bitter cold. Sometimes I plowed my way through several feet of freshly fallen snow, breaking a path in those early morning hours. And I was sleepy! Occasionally, when I reached the warm hall of an apartment house, I would lie down for a short snooze, awakening to find it was daylight.

Walt delivered his newspapers within a 24 square block area immediately north and just east of his home on 31st Street, (and later from his home on Bellefontaine Avenue) in a collection of streets known as the Santa Fe neighborhood. This area was ringed by Prospect Avenue on the west to Indiana Avenue on the east, and E. 27th Street on the north to E. 31st Street on the south.

While many of the homes were modest in nature, others were larger and reflected a degree of affluence. According to Walt...

"My route was in a wealthy neighborhood. After school I couldn't play like the other kids. I was excused a half-hour early for the papers. I could get up right in the middle of some boring subject and just walk out. Nobody could stop me. But when I'd go around at night, because I couldn't play, I'd come upon a bunch of schoolmates and they were playing out in one of the kid's yards, big yards. So I used to put my paper bag down and I'd play with them for a while. Then I'd have to get my paper bag on and go like the dickens to catch up.

I'd start off at 3:30 in the morning. Some of these kids had wonderful toys, and in the summertime, on the front porch, there'd be all of these toys. Things I didn't have. I didn't have any toys. Everything my parents gave me was something practical, something I needed, underwear. My brother Roy was always the one that saw that Ruth and I had a toy. And Roy didn't have much money. Roy was one of the kindest fellas I've ever known in my life to his family and other people. He's a very kind-hearted guy, although I think he's very mule-headed at times, too. (Laughing)

I'd go along in the morning and here a kid's toys (would) be out on these big porches. I'd put my paper bag down and go up and play with it...the wind up trains. I'd sit there and play all alone with it, you know? I remember one time I came to a porch and they'd been out there in the evening before...and sitting over here was a box of candy. So I sat there and ate candy and played with the toys (laughing). I always carefully put them back on the track in the same place so they wouldn't know I'd played with them. Then I'd have to run...to catch up.

It seemed like always in the wintertime, I was sleepy in the morning. For a while, I'd get up at three. On my route there were several apartments and they were all steam heated. I'd come a long there and I'd be so sleepy...I'd go up three floors and deliver to all the doors...and then I'd say (to myself), 'If I could just lay down for five minutes.' I'd wake up and it would be daylight and I couldn't remember whether I'd delivered the apartment.

You know, that period I went through as a newsboy...I've never forgotten. (T)o this day I have dreams that I've missed some customers on my route. I wake up and think, gosh I've got to hurry and get back - my dad will be waiting at that corner. I still dream that. It's the darndest thing. I remember those icy cold days, slidey (sic) and slippy (sic) and crying. I was so darned cold."

In all the many articles I've read about Walt and his newspaper route over the years, I've never read an article that included photos of the homes on his route, a detailed description of the neighborhood, or even an image of the newspapers he delivered from that time. The authors have always left those story elements up to the reader's imagination. I decided to change that.

In 1940, the city of Kansas City took photos of every home and business within the city limits for taxation purposes. To give readers a better understanding and visualization of this part of Walt's life, I decided to access this database of images and track down five photos of homes in the Santa Fe neighborhood, each built between 1905 and 1909, which together represent the kind of homes Walt delivered newspapers to on his route, 25 years prior. While they may or may not be the actual homes Walt and Roy delivered to, though it is very likely that they are, the following photos will allow you, *for the first time*, to have a more clearly defined sense of the actual route Walt walked and the kind of homes and porches he delivered newspapers to while making his rounds.

Photos courtesy of Missouri Valley Special Collections - Kansas City Public Library

Gertie the Dinosaur
& The Wonderland Theatre

Wonderland Theatre - Kansas City, MO

By age 13, Walt was captivated by the idea of animation, even to the point of neglecting his studies at the Benton Grammar School just so he could practice his drawing. Delivering the newspaper every day, he was probably thrilled to read that the "world's most famous cartoonist", Winsor McCay, had created a new and innovative animated film, titled *Gertie the Dinosaur*, and he was debuting the film to the world at Kansas City's Wonderland Theatre, of all places. With perhaps a nickel or a dime in his pocket for a ticket, Walt set out in late December of 1914 or early 1915 and made his way north a little under four miles to the theatre at 12th and Grand to see this new miracle in animation.

Drawing from the 1914 animated film "Gertie the Dinosaur"
Image courtesy of Billy Ireland Cartoon Library & Museum
- Ohio State University

When picturing Walt viewing *Gertie the Dinosaur*, I've always had to use my imagination to get a nebulous sense of his experience, as I had no idea what the theatre looked like, if it was located nearby in his neighborhood or across town, or if it was on a nicely landscaped boulevard or perhaps a crowded urban street. In uncovering the photo atop the previous page, however, it all came into view, as I discovered for the first time that the Wonderland Theatre was located on the corner of a busy downtown street bustling with activity, and for young Walt to get there from his home over on E. 31st Street he probably took a combination of electric trolleys, each loudly clanging a bell as they made their way through the busy traffic of the era.

Today, Walt's viewing of *Gertie the Dinosaur* at the Wonderland Theatre is recognized by the Walt Disney Company as being a seminal moment in Walt's life and his decision to become an animator.

ANIMATED CARTOONS BY E.G. LUTZ

A 1920 first-edition, complete with an extremely rare dust jacket
Author's Collection

The innovative *Gertie the Dinosaur* was part of a vaudeville act performed by Mr. McCay, in which he stood on stage and interacted with Gertie as she lumbered onto the scene and began to consume trees and rocks, responded to questions, and drank an entire lake. This film had such an influence upon Walt deciding to become an animator that Mr. McCay is acknowledged today by The Walt Disney Company with a couple of tributes secretly hidden by Imagineers in plain sight within Disneyland and Walt Disney World Resort.

While cartooning, in the form of comics and editorial newspaper cartoons, was wildly popular at the time, with Mr. McCay's *Little Nemo in Slumberland* and *Dream of the Rarebit Fiend* being widely read in newspapers all across the country, the art of animation was still in its infancy. As a result, there was little which Walt could use as a reference or teaching tool at the time to learn the craft, as well as the skills necessary to pursue his dreams.

In 1920, Walt partnered with his friend, Ub Iwwerks, to form a commercial art firm called Iwwerks-Disney, in which they produced ads for local businesses. This endeavor was short lived, however, and in 1921 Walt began creating animated films, which he called Newman Laugh-O-grams. During this period, Walt relied upon two early resources to learn and develop his animation skills; the *Motion Studies* volumes by Eadweard Muybridge, a pioneer filmmaker who studied and photographed the motion of humans and animals, and a new book, first published in 1920, titled *Animated Cartoons - How They Are Made - Their Origin And Development*, by E.G. Lutz.

Animated Cartoons was the first book to provide readers with extensive knowledge about the art and science of animation. Its pages provided Walt with lessons on how to capture the nuances of anatomy and movement, as well as the effects of motion upon a subject. In addition, it explained in detail the science of animation and the equipment used to create a moving motion picture from thousands of still images. It is often said that "It all started with a mouse.", but before that mouse, Walt's early skills as an animator started with this very book, which he relied upon to create the many characters that would launch his career and bring him worldwide success and prestige.

BERT HUDSON'S BARBERSHOP

Bert Hudson's Barbershop - Circa 1940 - The barbershop is on the far left of the photo, with the barber pole out front

Photo courtesy of Missouri Valley Special Collections

Whenever Walt walked down busy E. 31st Street to Benton Grammar School, he would pass by Bert Hudson's Barbershop, which was located about a block away from his home on Bellefontaine Ave., near the corner of Agnes Ave. and E. 31st. Walt and the owner, Bert Hudson, had developed a rapport, perhaps during discussions while Walt was getting his hair cut, and seeing his artistic talent, Bert began offering Walt either a free hair cut, or 10 or 15 cents, in exchange for regular drawings, which Bert would display in the front window and throughout the shop. This afforded Walt some degree of celebrity in the neighborhood, as the shop was soon filled with his work, and folks in the neighborhood would stop by regularly just to see what new work of art he had created. According to Neal Gabler's biography, *Walt Disney*, Walt stayed in touch with Bert over the years, writing in a note to him more than thirty years later... *"It was a great stimulant to me to know my efforts were appreciated, and boy, how I looked forward to the showing of that weekly - or was it monthly - cartoon in your shop."*

The Work of the Kansas City Slide Co.

As one reads about Walt and his days in Kansas City, the story typically follows a chronological progression where Walt works for the Pesmen-Rubin Commercial Art Studio, then forms Iwwerks-Disney Commercial Artists with Ub Iwwerks, followed by Walt answering a Want Ad placed by the Kansas City Slide Company. From there, he strikes out on his own again to form Laugh-O-grams Films, before ultimately leaving Kansas City in 1923 for Los Angeles, where his dreams begin to become a reality. In reading these story elements, I've always felt there was more to learn about Walt's time at the Kansas City Slide Company. If I did the research and uncovered new materials, would it be possible to capture and share the essence of what he felt when he was working at his desk, engaged in a conversation with his coworkers, or walking the hallways?

To attempt to do so, it is first important to understand the context of Walt's job. In the January 29, 1920 edition of the

Kansas City Star, there appeared an ad placed by the Kansas City Slide Company for a "First Class Man" who could create cartoons and wash drawings, the latter being a technique where a semi-transparent layer of color is applied in combination with a pen drawing on a glass advertising slide, in a manner similar to watercolor painting. Walt applied for the position and was hired. Ub Iwwerks would be hired soon afterwards.

So what was it that captured Walt's attention with this ad? Surely it wasn't about just collecting a paycheck. In scanning the hundreds of Help Wanted ads listed in the Kansas City Times and Kansas City Star newspapers from this era, I noticed that there were plenty of positions offered on a daily basis for delivery drivers, salesmen, messengers at local railroads, even phone operator positions at the Kansas City Star, a job that might have given Walt a foothold at the newspaper.

About this time, there were approximately 16,000 motion picture theatres of various sizes operating all across the United States, roughly half of which displayed advertising slides promoting national brands, as well as the products and services of local small businesses. When Walt saw the animated film *Gertie the Dinosaur* at the Wonderland Theatre in late 1914 or early 1915, he no doubt saw a number of these slide advertisements displayed before the film, during reel changes, or perhaps even as commercials or a one-minute "trailer" after the show, each likely produced by the Kansas City Slide Company. He may have also seen one of the Kansas City Slide Company's "motion picture" advertisements, which were simply individual slide images that used rudimentary stop-motion "animation", with each slide displaying the name *Kansas City Motion Picture Co.* on its bottom edge. If he didn't see them here, he no doubt saw them elsewhere while viewing other films in town. As a result, when Walt saw the Help Wanted ad placed by the Kansas City Slide Company, he was fully aware that they were producing "motion pictures" under the name of the Kansas City Motion Picture Co., making it one of the most promising opportunities in Kansas City for him to pursue his dreams of becoming an animator.

The Advent of Advertising Slides

Advertising slides were an extension of the common lantern slide. In the latter half of the 1800s, *the era just prior to the arrival of silent movies*, the most popular form of public entertainment was storytelling through the use of a "Magic Lantern" projector. This innovative technology cast a large image on a screen or wall by shining a light through a glass "lantern slide", which contained a static photographic or colored image on its surface. Magic lantern "theatres" were set up in small shops or homes, often in informal settings, and the public would pay to enjoy entertainment in the form of scenic, educational, or story-telling slideshows.

Magic Lantern - Circa 1880

By the time Walt was born in 1901, the magic lantern as a form of entertainment was widespread, but its days were quickly coming to an end, as an exciting new form of entertainment had arrived...the silent movie. By 1910, silent movies had become wildly popular all across the country, introducing such stars as Fatty Arbuckle, Gloria Swanson, Douglas Fairbanks, and a favorite of young Walt's, Charlie Chaplin. While the magic lantern's days were now numbered, the technology itself would quickly be adapted for use in the exploding number of silent movie theatres, as advertisers were anxious to pitch products and services to these captive audiences via advertising slide images.

A.V. Cauger Starts the Kansas City Slide Co.

A.V. Cauger
Photo courtesy of A. Scott Cauger, grandson of A.V. Cauger

In 1907, Arthur Vern Cauger lived in Granite City, Illinois, working as a "Jack Rabbit", that being one who showed short films in empty storefronts, set up with folding chairs and a simple curtain or sheet for a screen. Patrons would pay a nickel to watch a one-reel film lasting 15 to 20 minutes.

Seeing the fast-paced growth of silent movie theatres, Mr. Cauger moved to Kansas City, Missouri in 1909 and founded the Kansas City Slide Company at 1332 Grand Avenue. A year later, his new business was listed in the KCMO City Directory as the manufacturer of "Advertising Announcement and Song Slides", both of which were becoming more and more popular in silent movie theatres, with song slides being employed to encourage patrons to sing during reel changes, an activity that was very popular at the time.

Employees stuffing envelopes with copies of the KCSC Slide News
Photo courtesy of A. Scott Cauger, grandson of A.V. Cauger

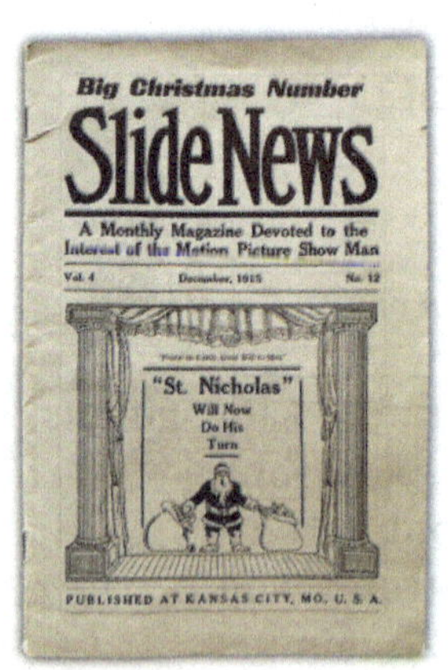

Using his business acumen in an increasingly crowded field of advertising slide manufacturers, Mr. Cauger began by offering slides locally, employing thirty-two employees by 1912. By 1914, his business had prospered, with now more than sixty employees offering advertising slides to clients nationwide, a base that would soon account for 75% of his business. He was also marketing his growing business via catalogs and a small monthly newsletter, titled *Slide News*, which typically featured 30 or more pages of articles, tips, and advice all related to the use of advertising slides in the world of motion picture theatres. In addition, the catalog offered hundreds of different slide designs available for order.

By 1915, he had grown the Kansas City Slide Co. into the largest mail-order advertising slide company in the country, offering countless choices of advertising slide designs, "expert work", and fast turnaround times. More importantly, he had his eye on the future, and was now offering his customers a selection of innovative new "motion picture" slides.

Between 1915 and 1920, the technology used for these "motion pictures", while cutting-edge, would change little, consisting of simple stop-motion techniques. Still, once Walt was hired in 1920, this basic technology would provide him with his first real experience in creating animation, and more importantly, the inspiration to follow his dreams.

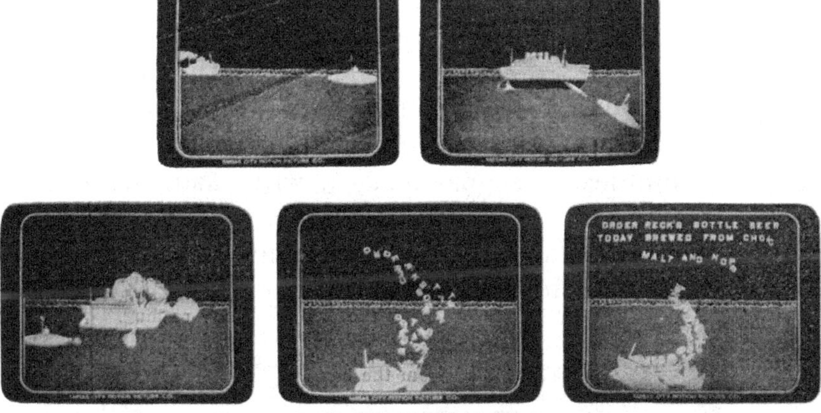

Stop motion advertisement example -
Kansas City Slide Co. "Animated Cartoons Advertising Films"
It's interesting to note that, as early as 1915, the small copy you see below each image references The Kansas City Motion Picture Co.

"I started, actually, to make my first animated cartoons in 1920. Of course, they were very crude things then and I used...oh sort of little puppet things. We didn't draw them like we do today. I used to make little cut-away things and joints were pinned and we'd put them under the camera and we'd maneuver them and we'd make him do things."

- *Walt Disney - Interview with Fletcher Markle - 1963*

Initially, Walt and Ub were both hired to illustrate advertising slides, but they were soon reassigned to creating motion picture slides and a new product called "movie trailers." These were one minute advertisements, typically consisting of 60 feet of film, which were added onto the end of motion picture reels, hence the name "trailers."

Choose From Hundreds of Designs

The Kansas City Slide Co. was large enough that many of its customers were under contract to automatically receive new slides on a weekly basis. No slide designing or order placement on the customer's part was necessary. For those who did order as needed, the process to order slides was pretty straightforward. Customers would receive in the mail from the Kansas City Slide Company a copy of their monthly *Slide News* newsletter, accompanied by a catalog and order form. From this they'd choose the slides they wanted in the quantities needed. Hundreds of different slide designs were available, including countless seasonal images, with many featuring a blank area in the main field where a customer's custom message could be placed, or at a minimum, a spot at the base of the slide for a customer's business name and location.

1719 Wyandotte Street, Kansas City 8, Missouri

Old Time Advertising Slides

Slides Pictured are Stock Slides. See Page 5 for Prices

Kansas City Slide Co. Catalog
Author's Collection

Stock "Announcement" slides, such as those that informed theatre patrons that there was to be no whistling, applause was appreciated, and those who spat on the floor would be arrested, were offered at a low price of $0.33 cents each. (As of 1915) Stock advertisements, including photographic slides "...on which NO CHANGE is desired EXCEPT the DEALER'S NAME", were priced at $0.50 cents, while illustrated slides with illustrations provided by the advertiser were priced at $0.75 cents. The Kansas City Slide Co. specialized in fast service, and with 90% of all orders being of a "Rush" nature, those slides received an extra "Special service charge" of $0.10 each.

The Production Process

As the largest mail-order advertising slide manufacturer in the country, the offices of the Kansas City Slide Company were humming with activity. As Walt sat at his desk or walked the hallways, he could no doubt overhear the conversations and corresponding work being done to receive order forms, create slides, package the orders, and get shipments out the door. Lunch breaks were probably filled with ongoing conversations amongst his colleagues about the different illustrations being created, how an order required a monotonous amount of detailed colorization, the mundane process of wrapping slides in their protective paper trim, and other details that filled the employees' day-to-day routines. Photos taken in 1913, approximately seven years prior to Walt's arrival, show offices in a bit of a haphazard state, with stacks of paper and supplies filling most every available shelf and space, no doubt because of how busy everybody was. This likely continued during Walt's employment, as well.

An illustrator paints a card for Brambach Baby Grand Pianos in front of windows diffusing bright ambient light. - Circa 1913
Photo courtesy of A. Scott Cauger, grandson of A.V. Cauger

The production process for an advertising slide began with an illustrator, such as Walt, sitting at his desk and using white paint to paint artwork and lettering onto a large piece of black card stock, typically 16 inches by 16 inches in size, though photographs offering more detail were also commonly used. Illustrators who were also proficient letterers, such as Ub Iwerks, were prized for their ability to quickly and skillfully create various typefaces, calligraphy, cursive writing, etc. all by hand, as generating quality copy was a slow process without today's modern tools. When creating their illustrations, Walt and his fellow illustrators followed a basic design principle which called for conveying the message in a pleasing and attention getting manner, while minimizing the amount of white paint used on the black background so as to not startle movie patrons with too bright of an image when the slide suddenly appeared on the screen in a darkened theatre.

When finished, the illustrated 16 inch by 16 inch card would then be photographed so as to create a glass plate with a negative image of the illustration. From this single negative, countless glass advertising slides could be generated, each now with a positive image.

A photographer photographs a positive image on card stock to create a glass slide negative. Circa 1913
Photo courtesy of A. Scott Cauger, grandson of A.V. Cauger

Prior to today's digital technology, thin lightweight film was used to create photographs. Camera film was introduced as cutting-edge technology in the early 1900s, thanks to the Eastman Kodak Company, and this was used for nearly 100 years, until the invention of the digital camera. (Note: Eastman Kodak was an early sponsor of Disneyland.) Before the introduction of film, however, photographs were captured on rigid glass plates, and these came in all sizes, large and small. The process, while labor intensive, was straightforward and involved two primary steps; the creation of a glass slide "negative", which in turn was then used to create one or more glass slide "positives". To create positive glass slide images from a negative slide at the Kansas City Slide Company, a photographer would open a box containing perhaps 100 blank glass slides, each pre-coated on one side with a thin layer of a silver gelatin emulsion. Depending upon how many duplicates he needed to create of the same design, he would remove the corresponding number of blank slides, and, one by one, overlay the negative glass slide atop them, with the silver gelatin emulsion side "sandwiched" between the two slides. Next, he would shine a bright light through the negative slide for a pre-determined amount of time, usually only seconds, onto the blank slide. This created a positive image on the layer of silver gelatin emulsion, though it was not visible to the naked eye at this point. To reveal the positive image, the photographer would then bathe the entire blank slide in a "developing" solution, causing the positive black and white image to slowly reveal itself. From here, the slide would be immersed in a solution which would permanently "fix" the image to the glass slide, before being cleaned and placed on a rack to dry.

Colorizing or "Washing" the Slide

An artist colorizes a glass slide announcing "No Smoking". Note the tray with multiple colors on her desk, as well as the paint brushes to her right. Circa 1913
Photo courtesy of A. Scott Cauger, grandson of A.V. Cauger

For many of the slides, the next step in the production process involved colorizing, or "washing", the slide. If color was desired on finished glass slides, for example to highlight certain words, dim a bright white background, or to give an item such as a dress or flower some color, then the slides would be hand-painted, or "washed", with the desired colors. If an order called for 25 slides, as an example, then an artist would have to perform the same colorizing steps for each of the 25 slides. Oftentimes, a single slide would include three or four different colors, making the task somewhat tedious.

Once the advertising glass slides were produced and colorized, they were then stored in stacks awaiting their next steps in the production process, that being customization, the application of a paper overlay promoting the Kansas City Slide Company, an overlay of a clear glass slide, and a final wrap of a paper strip to secure the two slides together and to protect the user from any sharp edges.

Customizing the Slides for the Client

The Kansas City Slide Company created hundreds and hundreds of "generic" slide designs for hats, dresses, shoes, automobiles, farm implements, and many, many other items, usually leaving a blank area within the main field of the design, or more commonly on the lower quarter of the slide image, which allowed for the slide to be "customized". Within this blank area, a thin strip of clear film with text promoting the company that ordered the slide would be overlaid. In the image seen here, the J.M. Welch & Son company ordered a generic advertising slide that promoted hats, and then had the Kansas City Slide Company affix their company name at the base of the slide using a clear strip so as to give the ad a more "local" presence. Companies could also have completely custom made slides created for an additional cost.

Final Production Steps

After a slide was ordered, colorized, and customized, a paper border promoting the Kansas City Slide Company and its catalogs or "Slides for Every Purpose" was applied to the face of the advertising slide. Next, a clear glass slide of the same dimension was overlaid atop the advertising slide image, so as to protect it. A paper strip was then glued, by hand, around the perimeter of the two slides so as to hold them together and to protect the user from the slides' sharp edges.

Employees wrapping glass slides with paper strips.
Circa 1913
Photo courtesy of A. Scott Cauger, grandson of A.V. Cauger

With glass slides now complete, they would then be carefully packaged in small corrugated cardboard boxes and in turn mailed to customers nationwide.

Kansas City Slide Co. slide and package - Circa 1925
Author's Collection

I would like to thank A. Scott Cauger, grandson of A.V. Cauger, for his generous contributions of rare 1913 images and historic information for this article.

Uncovering the Kansas City Slide Co.

Kansas City Slide Co. - 2449 / 2451 Charlotte Street
Photo courtesy of A. Scott Cauger, grandson of A.V. Cauger

If you're a fan of Disney history, you've no doubt seen the photo above many times, most likely taken in the spring of 1922. Walt is sitting atop a short wall adjacent to the entrance steps, while standing immediately to his left is A.V. Cauger, and further to his left is Ub Iwerks, wearing a vest and tie. Unfortunately, this building no longer stands today. However, a small yet important piece of it remains, and in 2024, I, along with A. Scott Cauger, the son of Ted Cauger and grandson of A.V. Cauger, had the good fortune to "rediscover" this piece.

When Walt responded to an ad in the January 29, 1920 edition of the Kansas City Star for a "First Class Man" who could create cartoons and wash drawings, he was responding to an ad placed by A.V. Cauger, who was advertising for more artists to help him deal with the continued growth of his Kansas City Slide Company business. In addition to hiring more personnel, he was also in the midst of building new offices and production facilities so as to move from his current location at 1015 Central Street in downtown Kansas City to 2449 / 2451 Charlotte Street, a few miles to the south. Here, a new brick building designed specifically for the needs of his business would allow him to more efficiently develop his advertising slides and films, improve their quality, and keep up with the increasing demand for his products and services. Inside, his artists, such as Walt and Ub, would find generous amounts of ambient natural light for their work, a specially built screening room, better production and shipping facilities, and specially designed fire proof vaults to hold the increasing quantity of stored film, which was highly flammable. Perhaps most importantly, however, this new building would more comfortably accommodate his growing staff, all of whom would begin each morning by passing through an entrance set beneath a large sign made of concrete, roughly 9' x 3' in size, which read *Kansas City Slide Co.* Much like the famed *Walt Disney Studios* sign situated atop Walt's offices on Hyperion Avenue in Los Angeles beginning six years later, which no longer exists today, the sign adorning the entrance of the Kansas City Slide Co. was historically significant, as this was the location where Walt Disney and Ub Iwerks created their very first works of animation. In fact, the entire Hollywood animation industry, including Frez Freleng, Rudolph Ising, Hugh Harman, and Bugs Hardaway, who created and introduced such animated characters as Bugs Bunny, Daffy Duck, Tweety, Porky Pig, and many others to generations of Americans, got its start in this very building.

Walt would pass under this sign every day when he went to work until the spring of 1922, when he would leave to begin his own business, Laugh-O-gram Studios, on nearby Forest and 31st Street. According to his grandson, Scott, in January of 1922, A.V. Cauger adopted two new company names; United

Film Ad Service, to serve his national business, and Kansas City Film Ad Service for his more local and regional business, with both names now reflecting his growing film services instead of his slide offerings. With this, the large Kansas City Slide Co. sign above the entrance was covered with a new sign just prior to Walt leaving, the one you see in the photo at the beginning of this article. Unfortunately, despite the earnest efforts of Dan Viets and Ted Cauger throughout 1998, the long unoccupied and now dilapidated building was razed in 1999.

So, whatever happened to the large concrete Kansas City Slide Co. sign? Did this important piece of Disney history meet the same fate as the Walt Disney Studios sign? Was it demolished and disposed of, perhaps taken to a landfill along with the rest of the bricks, iron, and glass of the Charlotte Street building? Thankfully, due to the vigilance, foresight, and actions of Dan Viets and Ted Cauger, along with Butch Rigby, the sign was saved, being removed just prior to the building's demolition. The question is...where is the sign now?

In June of 2024, A. Scott Cauger and I, acting on a lead Scott had received, drove to an abandoned grocery store on Troost Avenue in southeast Kansas City. We were on a hunt to find this unique piece of Disney-related history, *the very Kansas City Slide Co. sign that used to hang above the entrance to the Charlotte Street building.* We had heard the grocery store was being restored, having suffered a fire in its roof sometime ago, and the Kansas City Slide Co. sign was supposedly somewhere inside, kept there for storage and safekeeping by Butch Rigby. We pulled up to find a non-descript and long-neglected building with its windows painted over and its front door locked, giving the appearance that it hadn't been used in ages. Nobody answered the door when we knocked, so we walked around to the side of the building hoping to find another entrance. There, we found an open door and were greeted by a workman who was busy sandblasting fire damage off the interior walls of the store, while his partner was painting new iron support beams on a lift up above. We mentioned that we were in search of a historical sign, one that was out of place in this construction site, but tied to the history of Walt Disney and A.V. Cauger. The workman enthusiastically said he knew just what we were looking for, and he motioned to a large tarp covering something at the front of the store, next to the graffiti sprayed windows. With a sense of excitement, yet unsure of what to expect, we approached the tarp, grabbed a corner, and gave it a pull, ceremoniously uncovering three large sections of concrete that together spelled out...*Kansas City Slide Co.* What a thrill it was to see this! While its surroundings were less than dignified, the well-preserved sign had a sense of awe and, to a degree, majesty, proudly conveying its historical importance as it appeared there in that dusty work site, just as it did when Walt, Ub, and A.V. Cauger looked upon it over 100 years ago.

The plan is for this sign to be put on display and shared with fellow Disney historians at the Laugh-O-grams museum, which is being restored by Thank You Walt Disney, Inc. You can learn more at www.ThankYouWaltDisney.org

Walt Disney's Hyperion Studio Business Card

Recently, I sat down with fellow Disney and A.V. Cauger historian, A. Scott Cauger, to review his collection of photos, artifacts, and Walt Disney signatures. Typically, he has them stored in a safe deposit box, but for my visit, they were all laid out on a desk before me. We looked at a couple of menus from the Walt Disney's Studio Restaurant, each with a bold signature from Walt on the cover, a number of unpublished photos from the 1940s and 1950s featuring Walt, A.V. Cauger, and a group of well-known animators, Disney Studio drawings from 1958, and original letters signed by Walt to complete the set. What Scott shared next was amazing, to say the least, especially for a fan of Disney history.

Upon arriving in Los Angeles from Kansas City in 1923, Walt and Roy set up an animation studio in their Uncle Robert's garage. From here, they moved to space at the back of a real estate office before moving next door to 4649 Kingswell Avenue, where they operated the Disney Brothers Cartoon Studio. With his business beginning to gain momentum, in January of 1926 Walt moved to what would now be known as the Walt Disney Studio, located at 2719 Hyperion Ave. in Hollywood. In addition to his Silly Symphonies, it was here that Walt introduced Oswald the Lucky Rabbit in 1927, and more importantly Mickey Mouse in 1928, with Mickey taking the world by storm beginning with his ground-breaking sound cartoon, *Steamboat Willie.*

As I reviewed A. Scott Cauger's collection, he showed me individual pieces one by one, saving the best for last. With a casual, "Here, have a look at this.", he handed me an *original never-before-seen and perhaps only-one-of-its-kind* business card belonging to Walt Disney from his time at the Walt Disney Studio on Hyperion Avenue. Scott was surprised to find this stunning piece of Disney history at the bottom of a common file folder years ago. On the front of the card there appears an image of Mickey's classic hand-waving pose, along with the Walt Disney Studio name at the top, a bold "Mickey Mouse", the Hyperion Avenue address, and the very telling description of "Sound Cartoons". On the back, in what appears to be Walt's handwriting, he wrote the name and address of the Tec-Art Studio, located at 5360 Melrose Avenue in Los Angeles, as well as the phone number of a "Cartoon Studio", OL 3515.

At face value, this is simply an old business card which belonged to Walt, and that in itself is fascinating to see, but is there more to the piece? Could I uncover any clues that would reveal *when* Walt may have used the card, and perhaps more importantly *why* he wrote what he did on the back, revealing a bit about what was capturing his day-to-day attention nearly 100 years ago? The answer to both of these questions is...yes.

To begin interpreting the clues for solving this unique Disney history riddle, I first had to delve into and understand the card's historical context, one which revolves around the world of silent movies evolving into "talkies".

Though introduced using rudimentary means in 1894, silent movies slowly improved and became very popular as one of the leading forms of entertainment shortly after the turn of the century, with silent movie theatres springing up in towns large and small all across the country, reaching their height of popularity from 1910 through the mid-1920s. Of course the movies were silent, so to add excitement and drama to the films, theatres would employ a single piano player or a small orchestra, usually located in a pit at the front of the theatre, to play dramatic music timed with the visual action appearing on the screen, thus making the film far more entertaining and imbuing it with a sense of realism.

While the use of pianists and orchestras was an effective way to bring a movie to life, audiences at the time wondered what their favorite silent film stars sounded like, and they wished to hear them speak on the screen. The problem was there was no existing technology that would allow for this.

By the mid-1920s, numerous inventors and companies in America and Europe, including R.C.A., Warner Bros., Western Electric, and Tri-Ergon, were making progress in their efforts to bring synchronized spoken words, sounds, and music to silent films. They faced three substantial hurdles in doing so, however; perfectly synchronizing speech and sounds with the action appearing on the screen, producing those sounds with high-quality and fidelity, and lastly projecting all of this loudly enough to fill a theatre.

In the race to invent, patent, and create the leading sound synchronization technologies, two processes had emerged at the forefront of the inventors' efforts: sound-on-film and sound-on-disc, the latter being by far the more popular and economical process. With sound-on-disc technology, a compatible movie projector was fitted with a separate disc player, a device similar to the old record players, and the projectionist was tasked with dropping a needle on a spinning disc at the exact moment the film began, hoping the sound emitted from the disc would then perfectly synchronize with the action in the film. The downside with this technology was that if the projectionist erred in dropping the needle on the disc a bit too late or too early, the timing for any spoken dialog or sounds in the film, such as a slamming door, would be off or out of sync. In addition to the timing issue, the discs were usually made of fragile shellac, so if one was dropped by the projectionist during a disc change, (there were often four discs changed out during one feature length film) or maybe even broken in shipment on its way to the theatre, then the sound for the "talkie" was simply lost, and the audience's viewing experience was ruined.

The second emerging technology, sound-on-film, was less prevalent but more effective, yet also more expensive. With this process, spoken sound was recorded via a microphone as sound waves, which in turn were then converted into light waves that were then photographically inscribed onto the film itself as part of a single strip, thus ensuring any spoken words, sounds, and music were always synchronized to the action appearing on the screen for the length of the film.

In 1927, a little more than one year before *Steamboat Willie* premiered, Warner Bros. released *The Jazz Singer*, the first feature-length motion picture to successfully synchronize music and singing with action on the screen, a fascinating and mesmerizing feat that had never before been achieved. As a result of this stunning advancement in the film industry, all of Hollywood was now abuzz about adding sound to film. Suddenly, all the studios in town were building "sound stages", and new businesses sprang up overnight offering all kinds of sound-related services and products, including sound printing, sound ready preview rooms, sound-ready film, sound reproduction, and an abundance of other resources, all to meet the growing demand occurring all across the industry.

It's easy to think that Walt saw the success of *The Jazz Singer* and simply thought, "Hmmm, I should probably add sound to *Steamboat Willie.*", but always striving to be at the cutting edge of delivering quality cartoons, his was more of a strategic decision driven by the fast-paced groundbreaking changes he saw happening with sound all around him on a daily basis throughout the film and cartoon industry.

Deciphering the When and Why

With this historical context, we can now explore the clues for *when* Walt used his business card, as well as *why* he wrote what he did on the back.

The first clue appears on the front of the business card itself. On each side of the Mickey Mouse image appear the words "Sound" and "Cartoons". Walt and his studio didn't have any "sound cartoons" until he added sound to *Steamboat Willie,* beginning with his first attempt on September 15th in anticipation for the cartoon's premiere in New York on November 18th, 1928. As a result, if Walt designed and printed this card in *anticipation* of creating sound cartoons, then the earliest the card could be dated would be sometime in the summer of 1928.

At this point, we have the earliest probable year of the business card. Given Walt occupied the Hyperion address until 1940, when he moved to larger offices at his new Burbank location, then the latest we could date this card would be in 1940, thus creating a 12 year span for its existence. Fortunately, the notes Walt wrote on the back of the card offer up enough clues to narrow down this date range considerably.

The Tec-Art Studio

On the back of the card, Walt has written two things of interest. The first is the address for the Tec-Art Studio, located at 5360 Melrose Avenue in Los Angeles. Tec-Art Studio was a leading studio in Los Angeles that offered Hollywood film studios a variety of services, including "Recording, Settings, and Studio Facilities by contract". At the time, it was fully embracing the fast-growing sound-on-film technology, even going so far as to equip two new "huge" soundstages to meet the growing demand. *(Sound Waves magazine - March 1, 1929)*

So why did Walt write the address for the Tec-Art Studio on the back of one of *his* business cards? Seeing the exploding need for sound-on-film services, and in search of additional revenue, in early 1929 Walt and Roy created a new company, called the Disney Film Recording Corp., which offered film makers the same Powers Cinephone sound-on-film technology they employed when synchronizing sound to *Steamboat Willie*.

Photo used under license from Hollywood Historic Photos

In the April 15, 1929 edition of *Sound Waves* magazine, the following article announcing Walt and Roy's new business appeared on Page 3 of the periodical...

Disneys Form Sound Recording Co.

DISNEYS FORM SOUND RECORDING CO.,

-:- *Independent's Business Sought* -:-

The first mobile "sound on film" equipment for independent producers' use will soon make its appearance in Hollywood. It is being built for Walter and Roy Disney, producers for many years of animated cartoons. This sound unit was designed by William Garrity, the Disney chief engineer and George Loweree, his assistant, both DeForest experts.

According to Walter Disney, the entire outfit will be mounted on two trucks, the smaller of which will be available for direct contact with studio sets. The device has as its nucleus a Powers Cinephone, which records all sound direct on the film. A crew of pioneer sound on film experts will accompany the trucks. The Disney brothers, who will operate the device as the Disney Film Recording Corporation, are at present using the basic equipment to record sound for their current short subjects.

Ready Now

As we go to press, it is learned that this equipment is ready now. The major truck is of one and one-half ton capacity while the recording will be done on film, using the glow lamp process instead of the light valve. The Disney Brothers plan to do no producing of their own at present with the exception of the sound cartoons "Mickey Mouse" (1/2 reelers) six of these have been made already and are meeting great success.

The rental prices of the trucks have not been decided on at present, but a reasonable rental can be expected, it is said. Carl Stalling, as music director for the organization, is prepared to handle the music synchronization, composition, etc., necessary for independent units.

Article copy courtesy of the Margaret Herrick Library of the Academy of Motion Picture Arts and Sciences.

And the location they chose for their new Disney Film Recording Corp.?... a small office located at the **Tec-Art Studio, 5360 Melrose Avenue**.

Cartoon Studio OL 3515

The second note Walt wrote on his business card was "Cartoon Studio", accompanied by a phone number of OL 3515. According to a want ad that appeared in an April 1930 issue of *American Cinematographer* magazine, this is one of the phone numbers assigned to the Walt Disney Studio.

WANTED—To Buy: One Universal Camera, with dissolving shutter; 200 ft. magazine. Phone OL 3515 or GL 1295. Walt Disney Studio, 2719 Hyperion.

In Conclusion

Given Walt was entering the new, fast growing, and very competitive world of sound synchronization, it would make sense that he would want a professionally printed business card so as to make a strong first impression. That is not what we see here. Instead, Walt likely wrote the pertinent information necessary on the back of his existing Walt Disney Studio business card...prior to his new business cards being created. If this is the case, then it would date this card to sometime between the summer of 1928 (most likely) and December of 1929, when the Disney Film Recording Corp. was incorporated as a subsidiary of the Walt Disney Studio. So how did A.V. Cauger end up with the card? Perhaps Walt sent it to him thinking A.V. may be in need of the sound-on film services of Walt's nascent Disney Film Recording Corporation.

Inspiration for the Gas Street Lamps of Main Street, U.S.A.

Main Street, U.S.A. represents a time of exciting change at the turn of the 20th century. The whistles of steam-powered locomotives announce the arrival of the future in the American west, store front windows are filled with the latest fashions from around the world, and the flickering flames of gas street lamps are slowly being replaced with bright incandescent bulbs powered by the "new" electricity of the era.

In 1911, Walt's family moved to Kansas City, Missouri, where Walt's father, Elias, ran a business delivering the Kansas City Star newspaper. Required to help his father, 9 year-old Walt would rise at 3:30 a.m., leave the warm comfort of his home, and step out into the cold, dark mid-western morning to carry a heavy load of newspapers along his assigned route. Again, it's important to understand the historical context here. In 1911, few rural houses and neighborhoods were wired for electricity, and as a result, homeowners burned oil lanterns or candles for light, all of which were extinguished when they went to bed at night. Imagine Walt being 9 years old and he's standing on the sidewalk before dawn while on his newspaper route, perhaps at the corner of Benton Blvd. and E. 29th Street. As he looks down the block he's about to walk into, he doesn't see any electric street lamps or front porch bulbs illuminating his way, but instead only the dark intimidating shapes of houses situated amidst menacing tall elm and maple trees. Because his father requires him to place his newspapers behind the screen door of each home, he knows he has to walk into that enveloping darkness and make his way up onto one spooky front porch after another...all alone.

A gas street lamp in Walt's neighborhood - Circa 1940 Photo
Photo courtesy of Missouri Valley Special Collections - Kansas City Public Library

However, Walt had some help with his brave endeavors, for spaced throughout the neighborhood were tall gas street lamps, each, like a sentinel standing guard, burning brightly and piercing the cold darkness with a warm reassuring glow that would, however briefly, light his way as he passed beneath them.

As Walt was designing Disneyland more than 40 years later, he wanted to introduce guests to the magic of his new park by way of a nostalgic walk down Main Street, U.S.A. To make this experience as real as possible, he filled the street with an abundance of details large and small...horse-drawn carriages plied the street along with the new motorized jitneys of the era, the Disneyland News newspaper delivered the latest news of the day, and old-fashioned gas street lamps lined the way to lands of enchantment, adventure, the past, and the

future. Clearly, *something* in Walt's past had inspired him to include gas street lamps as part of the guests' experience on Main Street, U.S.A. instead of solely electric lights, which were readily available in 1955. I can't help but think that it was the gas street lamps that lit Walt's way in the dark while delivering newspapers as a boy in Kansas City that inspired him to line Main Street, U.S.A. in Disneyland with the same kind of lamps and comforting glow for his guests to enjoy.

Of note is that Walt's neighborhood was adorned with gas street lamps, and he would also pass numerous lamps while walking to Benton Grammar School from his home during the years of 1911 to 1917.

Of note, as well, is that the gas street lamps that line Main Street, U.S.A. today have a very similar, though not exactly the same, design as those found throughout Walt's neighborhood in Kansas City. (*Gas Street Lamp Photo - Kansas City - Circa 1940)*

Chapter Three

Eert & Ub Iwwerks In Kansas City

Ub and His Father's Lives in Kansas City

As you read about Walt's early life in Marceline and Kansas City, you learn about different aspects of Walt's stern father, Elias, and how he set the tone and course for the day-to-day lives of the Disney family. Like Walt's father, Ub's father, Eert Ubbe Iwwerks, also had a notable impact on shaping young Ub's life, albeit in a very negative manner, largely through his absence and, ultimately, the abandonment of his family.

Historical context is very important when understanding Disney history, as looking at it through today's contemporary lens shaped by our modern technologies and conveniences distorts the historical reality. As an example, it's easy to lose sight of the fact that Walt likely had to ready the horse and buggy now and again whenever the family rode into Marceline...when today all we have to do is push a button to start our cars. Without the historical context, we lose the sense of young Walt calmly approaching the horse, perhaps with a bit of hay in hand, placing the bridle and reins, and deftly hitching the wagon, all with the scent of a Marceline morning in the air.

To help understand more of the historical context of Ub's childhood, I've included information about Ub's father and aspects of his life in Kansas City in the following pages, much like you would read about Elias Disney. There is very little known about Ub's father, his family, and their lives during this period, but through some diligent research and a bit of luck, I'm pleased to present in the following pages some new and never-before-published information, from the discovery of Ub's "lost" childhood home and a photo of his father's barbershop to Eert's involvement in the Kansas City socialist party and never-before-seen examples of his photography.

THE DISCOVERY OF UB IWERKS' LOST CHILDHOOD HOME

It was in December of 1919 when two 19 year-old animators, Walt Disney and Ubbe Ert Iwwerks, met each other while working at the Pesmen-Rubin Commercial Art Studio in Kansas City, Missouri. In short order, they discovered that not only did they both share a passion for the craft and science of animation, but they also lived quite close to each other, less than 2½ miles apart. Theirs was a new friendship that would, ultimately, last a lifetime, as well as dramatically change the world of entertainment for many generations to come.

Ubbe Eert Iwwerks, who later changed his name to Ub Iwerks, is recognized as the "hand behind the mouse." Suffering a serious setback when the rights to his character Oswald the Lucky Rabbit were stolen from him by Charles Mintz in early 1928, Walt came up with the idea of a new character, one he would come to call...Mickey Mouse. It was Ub, however, who is credited with bringing Mickey Mouse to life on paper, and shortly thereafter animating Mickey's first cartoon, *Plane Crazy*, in its entirety, as well as many others.

From at least age 9 and through his teenage years, Ub lived with his family in a small home in Kansas City, Missouri. The belief amongst members of the Disney community is that his childhood home was a simple house built in the Craftsman style with a welcoming porch and front gable accented with three small windows, located at 2334 Hardesty Avenue.

2334 Hardesty Avenue, Kansas City, MO - Circa 1940
Missouri Valley Special Collections - Kansas City Public Library

However, through a lucky accident, and a good deal of persistent research, I have discovered that the house located at 2334 Hardesty Avenue *was not* Ub's childhood home, but instead his was the home located right next door, a portion of which you can see on the left side of the photo above.

A Lucky Accident

As a Disney historian, I collect Disney merchandise from the 1930s, as well as other pieces related to Disney history. Recently, I was fortunate to have stumbled upon and acquire an extremely rare and exciting piece of Disney history tied to Ub. I use the word "stumbled" because initially I wasn't aware of what I had found. As you can imagine, it was exciting to discover something that, at first glance, gave the impression to be insignificant, but then began to slowly reveal a unique Disney mystery, one which appeared to be of some importance. As if we are boarding a Disneyland attraction, join me in experiencing a magical moment, as we discover how a rare yet simple antique postcard led to an important historical Disney revelation!

For Sale: "Real Photo Postcard" Taken in Kansas City, MO

Above is an image of a postcard recently offered for sale online. When it first came to my attention, I didn't give the piece much thought. In fact, I nearly passed on it, as I don't collect postcards, nor do I know much about the world of collecting them. With its unremarkable description reading *"Real Photo Postcard" taken in Kansas City, MO*, it appeared to be simply a run-of-the-mill family photo of unknown folks sitting on the porch of a home somewhere in Kansas City, the kind of old photo one would find by the handful scattered about in a box at the back of an antique store. However, it was then that something caught my eye. In looking at the promotional copy found on the left edge of the postcard, I realized it read...

E. U. Iwwerks
Out Door Photographer
2336 Hardesty Avenue, K C MO.

It turns out this was no ordinary postcard, but instead it was a "real photo postcard" created by Ub's father, Eert Ubbe Iwwerks, over 110 years ago, no doubt as part of his out door photography business. I bought the postcard, happy to own a rare and obscure Disney-related artifact.

It was here that this story could have ended, but the postcard seemed to have a story of its own, one it was anxious to tell, as it slowly began to reveal an intriguing Disney mystery.

The Mystery…
Where Is/Was 2336 Hardesty Ave.?

Beginning in the early 1910s, Ub's father ran a business as an "Out Door Photographer", traveling throughout the area taking photos, perhaps with Kodak's new portable 3A folding pocket camera, which would, via the darkroom process, produce single or small quantities of real photo postcards. On the edge of each postcard Eert created, he would include his business address of 2336 Hardesty Ave. K.C., MO.

In doing some additional research, I found that within Eert's Naturalization papers, as well as the 1910 Census, both of which were official government documents, he listed his home address as being *2336 Hardesty Ave., Kansas City, Missouri*, signing the documents so as to indicate that the information he provided was accurate and true.

UNITED STATES OF AMERICA

DECLARATION OF INTENTION

Invalid for all purposes seven years after the date hereof.

United States of America, ss: In the District Court of the United States

I, Ert Ubbe Iwwerks, aged 61 years, occupation Photographer, do declare on oath that my personal description is: Color White, complexion Fair, height 5 feet 6½ inches, weight 134 pounds, color of hair Gray, color of eyes Brown other visible distinctive marks None

I was born in Uttum, Germany on the 28th day of June anno Domini 1855; I now reside at 2336 Hardesty, Kansas City, Missouri

I emigrated to the United States of America from Bremen, Germany

Eert Ubbe Iwwerks' Naturalization Record
March 27, 1917

In other words, Eert Ubbe Iwwerks' business address, 2336 Hardesty Avenue, was also his home address. By extension, this means that Ub Iwerks' childhood home was located at 2336 Hardesty Avenue, not 2334 Hardesty Avenue, the address for the simple craftsman style home. Mystery solved!

Not quite.

With this information, I then conducted a search online to find 2336 Hardesty Avenue. Oftentimes, homes as old as these have been replaced over time with a strip mall, a laundromat, or perhaps even a parking lot, but in this case my online search for the address of 2336 Hardesty Avenue determined that no such address exists! Only 2334 Hardesty Ave., the home many believe to be Ub's childhood home, and, immediately next door to the south, 2340 Hardesty Ave., an old white boarded up home in a restaurant parking lot, with not enough room for 2336 Hardesty Avenue to have ever existed between them.

So where is, or whatever happened to, Ub's childhood home at 2336 Hardesty Avenue?

At this point, I was stumped. Additional searches regarding Ub's childhood home or its address turned up absolutely nothing. Were the online maps incorrect, or had one of these two homes been assigned a new address at some point during the past one hundred-plus years? I had a feeling the answer to this mystery was buried deep in a historical archive somewhere, perhaps in the form of a simple notation on a building permit from the turn of the prior century, or maybe an old photograph that just happened to catch some house numbers in the background.

My research led me to two fascinating resources; Missouri Digital Heritage, which had an archive of photos showing every single home and business in Kansas City in 1940, and the Kansas City Public Library, whose team was especially helpful in finding and providing me with key documents.

With these resources, I set out to find the one document that would provide the incontrovertible proof I needed of the existence of Ub's childhood home at 2336 Hardesty Avenue, and, after a good deal of time and effort, that proof arrived one day in the form of a 1925 plat map from the Kansas City Public Library, a map which indicated that for a number of years the home located today at 2340 was assigned two addresses; 2340 Hardesty Ave. and...*2336 Hardesty Ave.!*

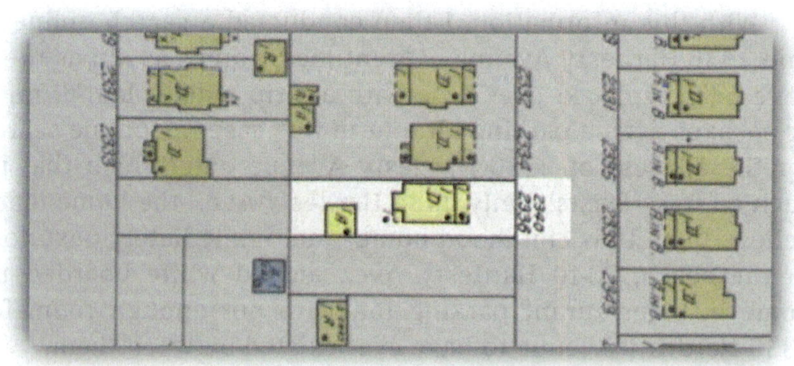

1925 Kansas City Plat Map -
Indicating one home assigned with the addresses of both
2340 Hardesty Ave. and 2336 Hardesty Ave.

Ub Iwerks' childhood home had been found!

With that, this Disney-related mystery was solved! And to further confirm these results, additional research revealed that the home located at 2334 Hardesty Avenue was not built until 1922, when Ub was 22 years of age, whereas the home at 2336 / 2340 Hardesty Ave. was built in 1900.

Ub Iwerks' childhood home
Located at 2336 / 2340 Hardesty Ave. - Photo Circa 1940
Missouri Valley Special Collections - Kansas City Public Library

Ub Iwerks' childhood home as it appears today

INSIDE UB IWERKS' CHILDHOOD HOME

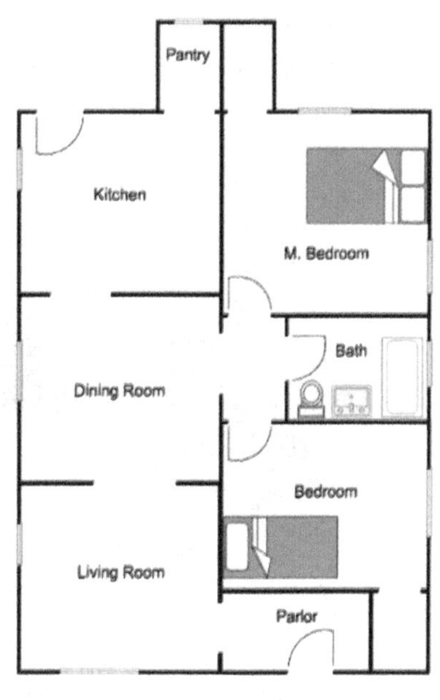

You'll be pleased to know that Ub's childhood home is still standing, boarded up in a restaurant parking lot on Hardesty Avenue. After discovering the home, my first thought was probably the same as yours... "What's it look like inside?" I have visited the home on two occasions, gaining access to inspect its main floor, basement, and attic. Entering through the front door, you step into a small parlor. A wall directly in front of you leads you left into a living room brightened by a large picture window. Turning to the right, you begin to make your way further into the house, entering the dining room. Here, a cast iron wood burning stove in the northwest corner of the room provided a single source of heat for the entire house back when Ub lived here, its stovepipe entering the chimney up near the ceiling. There is no fireplace. If you continue straight, you'll pass through a narrow door into the kitchen, with its pantry just to the right of the backdoor of the house. Returning to the living room, you'll turn left to find a short hallway running east and west, with the larger master bedroom to the left, and what was likely Ub's room to the right, at the front of the house. From the hallway, you access the bathroom, which held a sink, a toilet, and likely a short clawfoot tub against the north wall of the house. All of these features, as well as the wood stove, lights, doors, cabinets, and anything else of value, are now missing. The attic is empty with no flooring. Standing on the rafters, you can see the lath and plaster that make up the ceiling below. The basement is empty, as well, and all of its walls are made up of stacked limestone with mortared joints. There is no concrete, save for the damp floor, crisscrossed with grooves to move moisture to a drain.

The home has been unoccupied for quite some time, and as a result, its interior is in need of substantial repair and restoration. Small sections of the original wallpaper peek through in places on its lath and plaster walls, and much of its original dark-stained trim is still in place. Painted hardwood floors run throughout the house, but a leak in the roof has allowed water to enter the structure for a number of years, and, as you can imagine, this has caused some problems.

Hopefully, good fortune will shine on Ub's childhood home once again, and fans of Disney history will be able to step inside to see the home Ub lived in when he was growing up in Kansas City and spent time with Walt Disney, his friend who lived only a couple of miles away.

A New Aspect Of Ub Iwerks' Early Childhood Years

An extremely rare 1900 E. U. Iwwerks "Cabinet Card" promoting his pedigreed Light Brahmas.
Author's Collection

This story is about how a never-before-seen 125 year-old "cabinet card" featuring a chicken brought to light not only a heretofore unknown aspect of Ub's father's life, but by connecting the dots, revealed a previously unknown element of Ub's early childhood, as well.

As you peruse various sources of Disney history, you'll find that very little is known about Ub's early years, unlike Walt's, since so little information is available about this period in his life. Typically, biographies will highlight his contentious relationship with his father, who abandoned Ub and his mother in Ub's early teenage years, before progressing to explain how he went on to meet Walt at age 19.

Ub was born over 120 years ago, in 1901, and as a child, he grew up in a world dramatically different than ours today. The automobile was only a rumor at the time, so the dirt roads in his southeast Kansas City neighborhood were plied by horse and buggies. Vast corn fields stretched to the horizon in the Missouri countryside, and large red barns anchoring abundant hay fields were a common sight. And as in Marceline, the loud whistles of chuffing steam engines would announce their travels on the rails somewhere in the distance.

Unfortunately, many families in Missouri and across the country at that time were struggling just to make ends meet, and the Iwwerks family was one of them. You'll often read that Ub's father worked at four different occupations: a photographer, artist, and inventor, with the majority of his income coming from his steady work as a barber. However, in poring through some periodicals from that era, I discovered that he held yet another job in this agrarian economy, one where he sold chickens and eggs, which was a very common way for people to supplement their income at the time. In fact, if you were to peruse the Want Ads in the Kansas City Star around the time Ub was born, you'd see an abundance of ads touting chickens, eggs, or both for sale, with every ad claiming to offer the finest quality products in all of Kansas City.

EGGS—A $3 Setting for $1.50.

Iwwerk's non-setting pedigreed Light Brahmas.

A hatch will convince you as to square dealing, and the grown chicks as to the high quality of my stock—there are none better.

Twenty-one years experience as a breeder of standard-bred poultry.

E. U. Iwwerks, 1300 Union Ave., Kansas City, Mo.

An ad Eert Iwwerks ran for his pedigreed Light Brahmas in the April 26, 1899 edition of The Farmers Advocate.

Beginning sometime in 1878, which was 23 years before Ub was born, Eert began to develop an interest in breeding Standard-Bred poultry, that being breeds that have been officially recognized by the American Poultry Association. He would go on to breed prize-winning pedigreed hens over the next three decades, especially Light Brahmas, of whose eggs he claimed were... *"the largest of any breed known, rich and of a very delicate flavor."* His involvement in this community was so extensive that in August of 1900, he was elected as President of the Kansas City Fancy Poultry Breeders Association.

The discovery of Ub's father's extensive involvement with breeding chickens not only provides a new perspective on the day-to-day activities of the Iwwerks family, but it reveals for the first time an entirely new aspect of young Ub's life, as well.

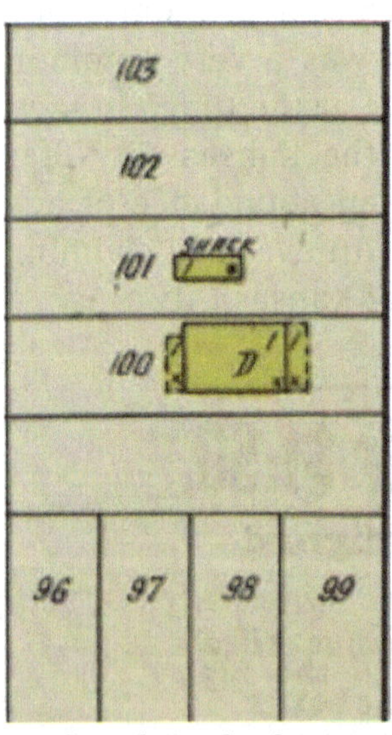

Ub's childhood home on Kansas City's Hardesty Ave. was located in a somewhat rural area, with few other houses nearby. In a way, it was a small farm-like setting. Given money was tight, it is likely that Eert ran his business of breeding and raising chickens from his own yard. In fact, I uncovered an early plat map from that time which indicates there was a small narrow unpermitted "shack" next to the Iwwerks' home, which would likely have been Eert's chicken coop. Given he was working five different jobs, it's also likely that he didn't have time to tend to his chickens, and with Ub being an only child, one can logically assume that daily responsibility fell upon him. If this is the case, then we learn for the first time that while Walt was delivering newspapers a couple of miles away, young Ub was likely feeding his father's chickens, collecting their eggs, cleaning the coop, and even helping with deliveries.

IWWERKS ART SERVICE

You'll commonly read that when Walt and Ub agreed in February of 1920 that Walt should leave their Iwwerks-Disney Commercial Artists venture to take a job at the Kansas City Slide Company, Ub would stay on and try to keep Iwwerks-Disney Commercial Artists afloat. However, while doing some research, I uncovered something that indicates this common Disney narrative appears to be an incorrect assumption.

In checking the pages of a March, 1920 newspaper published by the Chamber of Commerce of Kansas City, I discovered a small never-before-seen ad placed by Ub for Iwwerks Art Service. Since this is not an ad for Iwwerks-Disney Commercial Artists, this would strongly suggest for the first time that, instead of continuing to work at Iwwerks-Disney on his own, Ub instead started his own venture, offering from an office at 203 Railway Exchange Building...

"Illustrations - Designs - Lettering -
Posters & Art Work for General Advertising"

EERT IWWERKS' BARBERSHOP

Like Walt's father, Ub's father held a number of different jobs over the course of his life. While breeding hens on the side, he also worked as a barber, a job he would hold until he became an out door photographer sometime in the early 1910s. In the world of Disney history, you'll find very little about him being a barber, usually just a mention of it, perhaps along with a comment that he was also a "...photographer, skilled artist, and inventor."

As a Disney historian and researcher, I enjoy uncovering pieces of information which have never before been documented or published, particularly within the Disney community. While investigating Walt Disney's and Ub Iwerks' lives in Kansas City, I realized I may have stumbled upon the opportunity to discover and share another unknown piece of Disney history, this time with a photograph.

Through the course of my research, I obtained an address tied to Ub's father and dated to 1906, one which I had not seen before. Not being his Hardesty Avenue home address, I didn't know if it belonged to the Kansas City Fancy Poultry Breeders Association, the office of the City Central Committee of the Socialist Labor Party, of which he was a Chairman, or the address of the barbershop where he worked. If it was the latter, then this address may lead me to the discovery of something perhaps nobody has ever seen before within the Disney community...a photo of Eert Iwwerks' barbershop.

I began scouring a digital database containing thousands and thousands of photos taken of every single residence and building in Kansas City during 1940, a project the City had undertaken at the time for taxation purposes. Despite the numbering system being a bit backwards, I was eventually able to narrow my search to a collection of approximately 40 small thumbnails that should contain a photo of the address in question. I could see that most of the thumbnails were residences of all sizes and designs, but one particular image appeared to be of a small wooden building. What was I going to find when I opened this image and enlarged it? Would it be a home, a garage, a gas station, a retail store, or...would I find a photo of Eert's barbershop? I clicked on the thumbnail and slowly zoomed in to discover it was clearly a business on a busy street, and there, right by the front door, was a classic barber pole advertising the stylish hair cuts offered inside.

I had found Eert Iwwerks' barbershop.

While the photo was taken in 1940, I can't help but think that the building looked largely the same back in 1910 when Eert would leave his home on Hardesty Avenue and make his way west, perhaps on foot or by horse and buggy, for 13 blocks along 24th Avenue to the barbershop, where he'd practice his craft, probably spending much of the day extolling the beauty of his prize-winning Light Brahmas, doing his best to recruit members for the Socialist Labor Party, or showing off his new camera for the out door photography business he was going to start one day.

EERT UBBE IWWERKS - OUT DOOR PHOTOGRAPHER

Ub Iwerks' father, Eert Ubbe Iwwerks, is considered to have been a man of poor character and moral fiber, abandoning Ub and his mother when Ub was just a teenager living in Kansas City, leaving them destitute and to fend for themselves. As a result, Ub detested his father and never spoke of him, their relationship being so bereft of emotional attachment that upon learning of his death, Ub is reported to have said..."Throw him in a ditch."

While he was a poor father, his actions, be they positive or negative, likely influenced Ub's interests and who he would ultimately become. Eert Iwwerks' creative abilities were well known, as he had developed a reputation as a skilled painter of landscapes and nudes. He also possessed musical talent, sitting down on occasion at an upright piano to play popular songs of the era. Ub, in his later years at the Walt Disney Company, displayed a mastery of technical problem solving, perhaps influenced by another of his father's skillsets. As an inventor, the elder Iwwerks was granted three different patents by the United States Patent & Trademark Office, one of which employed a small cello-like instrument with a stylus, which would rest upon a turning record to produce a sound that was richer and clearer than that produced by the limited technology of the gramophones and record players of the day.

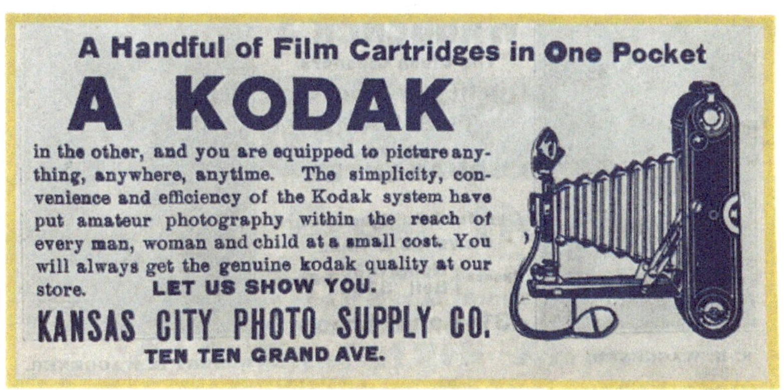

Kodak camera ad
From a 1914 Kansas City Electric Park souvenir brochure
Author's Collection

Aside from his creative and technical interests, Eert Iwwerks held a number of different jobs, and sometime during the early 1910s he began operating a business as an "Out Door Photographer", likely using Kodak's revolutionary 3A Folding Pocket Camera to take photos of different clients. Eert would then develop the film in a darkroom, probably located somewhere within his home at 2336 Hardesty Avenue, ultimately making one to perhaps a dozen or more copies as "Real Photo Postcards", which he'd then sell to the client who commissioned his work. In turn, the client would pass the cards out to family members, if it was a family portrait or something similar, or perhaps use them as advertisements for his or her own business, if the subject of the photo reflected their product or service. Cards such as these were an extremely popular form of advertising at the time, and would continue to be so until radio became more widespread during the 1920s.

Copies of the real photo postcards he created are difficult to find today, and there are only a few known surviving pieces, as they were made only of paper cardstock and are now more than 110 years old. What follows are four extremely rare examples of Eert Iwwerks' postcards, two of which are revealed here for the first time ever...

E. U. Iwwerks Postcard - Circa 1914
Author's Collection

This never-before-seen postcard from 1914 appears to be of three generations of a family posed on the front porch of a home in Kansas City, Missouri. With Kodak's new portable camera, it was common for photographers, such as Eert, to offer to take family portraits at customers' homes, which were not only less expensive, but also more convenient to arrange than a formal sitting in a photography studio across town.

If this was a family portrait photo, then Ub's father would have sold this one postcard, or multiples if he made them, to the family seen here. As an option, he may have photographed this family and then made multiple copies of the postcard to use himself as a promotional tool for his out door photography business and portrait taking skills. Note his promotional copy and address on the left edge of the image.

E. U. Iwwerks Postcard - Circa 1913
Author's Collection

Another never-before-seen E.U. Iwwerks postcard, the photo above displays what appears to have been a common subject for Eert, an ice man and his delivery wagon.

At the time this photo was taken, in approximately 1913, harnessed electricity was still a relatively new invention, with the majority of American families waiting for power lines to be strung to their residential neighborhoods and rural homes. As a result, it was common to see ice men and their horse drawn wagons on a daily basis plying their routes to deliver ice to their customers' homes, for each had what was called an ice box, a large wooden cabinet with two or three metal lined compartments, one of which held a large block of ice that would keep the perishables stored inside cold and fresh. As the ice block slowly melted over the course of a day or two, a homeowner would place an Ice Card in the front window of their home, and the ice man would then stop and deliver what the homeowner needed, which was typically between 25 lbs. to 100 lbs. of ice.

E. U. Iwwerks Postcard Photo - Circa 1913

From the collection of Michael Bushnell -
Publisher, Kansas City's Northeast News - Kansas City, MO.

Above, we see two more one-of-a-kind Real Photo Postcards produced by E.U. Iwwerks, both of which feature delivery wagons, the second of which hauled ice for the City Ice & Storage Company. Note the different style of promotional copy Eert used on the right edge of the postcards.

Chapter Four

The Early History of Disney Merchandise

The Early History of Disney Merchandise

1934 Colson Mickey Mouse Velocipede
Author's Collection

Of course, a trip to the Disney theme parks isn't complete without the perfect souvenir. Walk along Main Street, U.S.A. and you'll discover store after store and shelf after shelf filled with Mickey Mouse ears, colorful apparel, soft plush characters, toys of all kinds, tasty food treats, and hundreds of other fun items all featuring your favorite Disney characters.

The early history leading to all of this merchandise is a story as old as Mickey Mouse himself, and, as Walt said, it was all started by a mouse...on a children's writing tablet.

1929 - Mickey Mouse Children's Writing Tablet

In 1929, about one year after the release of Mickey's third cartoon, *Steamboat Willie*, the affable and adventurous star was beginning to take the world by storm, and while his popularity soared, Walt was focused on creating Mickey's next cartoon adventure, as well as running his growing business. As a result, Walt and his brother Roy hadn't given much thought to the idea of merchandising Mickey Mouse or any of their growing collection of Disney characters, but that changed in late 1929 when Walt was approached by a man while in a New York hotel lobby who offered him $300 for the rights to put an image of Mickey Mouse on the cover of a writing tablet for children. In an interview years later, Walt recalled... "*As usual, Roy and I needed money, so I took the three hundred.*" And with that, the very first Disney merchandise item was created.

Extremely Rare 1930 Mickey Mouse Children's Composition Book
Note how it opens right to left, versus bottom to top
Author's Collection

1929 - Walt Disney Enterprises

Unfortunately, the name of the man who approached Walt has been lost to history, but his timing played an important role in Walt's continued success, for in August of 1929 the Great Depression struck, sending America into economic turmoil almost overnight. The stock market crashed, bank accounts simply vanished, and countless businesses large and small all across the country were forced to close. Walt was fortunate, however, for his new character, Mickey Mouse, was growing more and more famous by the day around the world, and this new opportunity created by merchandise sales would add a timely and much needed revenue stream to his business. On December 16, 1929 Walt and Roy created Walt Disney Enterprises, and through this new division they would manage the growing sales and licensing of Disney merchandise.

1930s Borgfeldt 5" Fun-e-Flex Wooden Doll & Borgfeldt Letterhead
Author's Collection

1930 - Disney's First Licensing Agreement

Only a couple of months later, on February 3, 1930, Roy signed Walt Disney Enterprises' first licensing agreement with the Geo. Borgfeldt Corporation. Located in Manhattan, which was the center of merchandise licensing and distribution, the large Borgfeldt Corporation brought to the table 53 years of experience. Soon, they were offering retailers "the most unusual and complete line of Mickey Mouse and other Disney character merchandise", including bisque figures, wooden "Fun-e-Flex" figurines, handkerchiefs, tea sets, and more.

1932 – Walt and Roy Meet Kay Kamen

While the Geo. Borgfeldt Corporation lit the boiler of the locomotive that would pull the train of Disney merchandise, it was a former hat salesman who would stoke the boiler and run that train down the tracks and across the globe with a full head of steam.

Herman "Kay" Kamen was a 40 year-old merchandising executive with an office in Kansas City, Missouri, the same town Walt had left nearly a decade earlier to join Roy in Los Angeles and start the Disney Brothers Cartoon Studio. Kay had experience developing and selling merchandise based upon the Our Gang series produced by Hal Roach, and, seeing the limited reach of Disney's products in the hands of a small number of different distributors, he felt he could do a much better job of merchandising Walt's growing collection of characters. Full of confidence, he reached out to Walt and pitched the idea of having him become the sole representative for Walt Disney Enterprises. Intrigued by Kamen's pitch, Walt told him to drop by the studio to discuss the idea the next time he was in California. Kamen was a bold, creative, and innovative thinker, and he knew that he had to make an even stronger pitch in Los Angeles to capture the business of the company behind one of the world's most popular stars, Mickey Mouse. Withdrawing his life's savings and sewing it into the lining of his jacket, he boarded a train for the two day trip to Los Angeles, making sure not to fall asleep along the way, lest someone steal his hidden cash.

Arriving at the studio, Kamen explained his idea in detail to Walt and Roy, promising not only a substantial increase in business and revenue through the use of new and innovative sales and merchandising techniques, but also a commitment to ensuring that all Disney products produced under his charge would reflect only the highest standard of quality. Laying his life's savings out on the table to buy the rights to the position, he told them, "*I don't know how much business you're doing, but I'll guarantee you that much business, and give you 50% of everything I do over.*" After hearing his pitch, Walt and Roy excused themselves and stepped aside to have a private conversation between the two of them, where they agreed that Kamen's proposal would seamlessly fit with what they had in mind for the still nascent Walt Disney Enterprises. Turning around to inform him that he had a deal, they found him fast asleep, the result of having stayed awake for the past two days!

After mulling over the details for a few days, Walt and Roy signed the former hat salesman to a contract on June 29, 1932, and when the Borgfeldt contract expired, Kamen signed a deal on July 1, 1933 making him the sole licensing representative for Disney character merchandise worldwide.

The deal the Disney brothers struck with Kamen began not only a very profitable relationship, which ushered in innovative new ideas that generated millions of dollars in global sales, but also a warm friendship between the three of them that would continue for many years.

1934 Emerson Mickey Mouse Radio - Model 411
with extremely rare original box
Author's Collection

1933 – Kay Kamen Incorporated

Kay was a man who knew where he wanted to go and how to get there. Come the following year, he had opened Kay Kamen, Inc. in New York so as to be in the heart of the action near the offices of major merchandise manufacturers and importers. With the support of his staff of 20 sales representatives and in-house artists, he negotiated the deals, built the relationships, and provided the sales materials that would double Disney's merchandise sales to over six million dollars within only six months. Soon, department stores, toy stores, five and dimes, boutiques, bookstores, and countless other retailers across the globe were generating profits amidst the grip of the great depression from the sale of hundreds of different kinds of Disney merchandise items, including figurines, toys, stuffed dolls, furniture, apparel, school supplies, radios, record players, books, tablets, and more.

1934 Disney / Kay Kamen, Ltd. Catalog - First Edition
Author's Collection

1934 - Mickey Mouse Merchandise Catalogs

Kay Kamen was not only driven, he was also an innovator, and one of his early innovations was the introduction of his first Mickey Mouse Merchandise catalog in 1934, the "first of its kind in the history of merchandising." Filled with 76 pages of products produced by 49 different licensees, the catalog offered a wealth of Mickey Mouse branded items, including savings banks, sheepskin moccasins, toothbrushes, pop-up books, bisque figurines, tricycles, canvas shoes, and much more, all promoted with compelling black and white photographic detail.

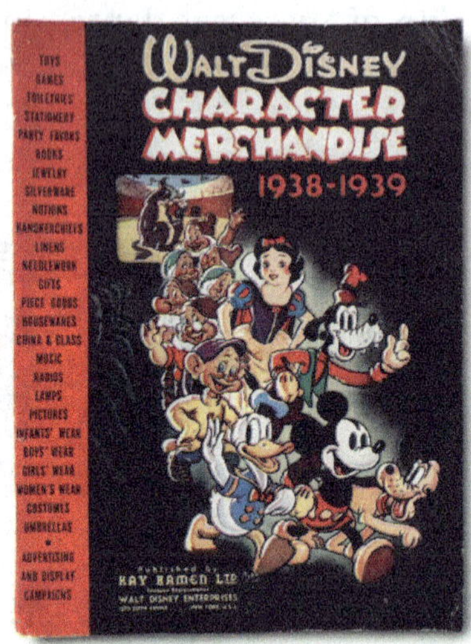

1935 and 1938 - 1939 Walt Disney Merchandise Catalogs
Published by Kay Kamen Ltd.
Author's Collection

This first catalog proved to be extremely successful, and it quickly became a driving force in placing Mickey Mouse and other Disney character merchandise in thousands of retail stores throughout America and around the world, generating a total of $35 million in sales by 1935. Because of its success, Kamen continued to publish additional catalogs on a yearly basis until 1949, when, sadly, he and his wife were killed in a plane crash on the Azores archipelago in the mid-Atlantic while returning to the United States from Europe.

Kay Kamen's Walt Disney Merchandise Catalogs

1947 - 1948 Walt Disney Character Merchandise catalog
Front and back covers - Author's Collection

Kay Kamen's merchandise catalogs are quite rare today. They don't come available for sale very often, and when they do, they usually command a price of between $1,000 to $2,000 each, depending upon their condition. As a result, it's not often that Disney history fans get a look inside to see the many different Disney merchandise products that were being offered more than 90 years ago. I'm fortunate to own a few different catalogs, and I'd like to share some of the actual pages and merchandise items with you here, complete with their classic 1930s black and white photography.

DOLLS

THE snappiest, most diversified line of world-famous Walt Disney character dolls that Knickerbocker has ever presented—stuffed dolls and wood composition dolls—headlined by those dynamic sales-getters, Mickey Mouse and Donald Duck in various costumes—to retail from $1.00 up.

KNICKERBOCKER TOY
COMPANY, INCORPORATED
200 Fifth Avenue,
New York, N. Y.

– 46 –

Knickerbocker Toy Company Dolls
1938 - 1939 Walt Disney Character Merchandise Catalog

Ingersoll Watch Company
1934 Mickey Mouse Merchandise Catalog

Mickey Mouse Movie Projector
Keystone Manufacturing Company
1934 Mickey Mouse Merchandise Catalog

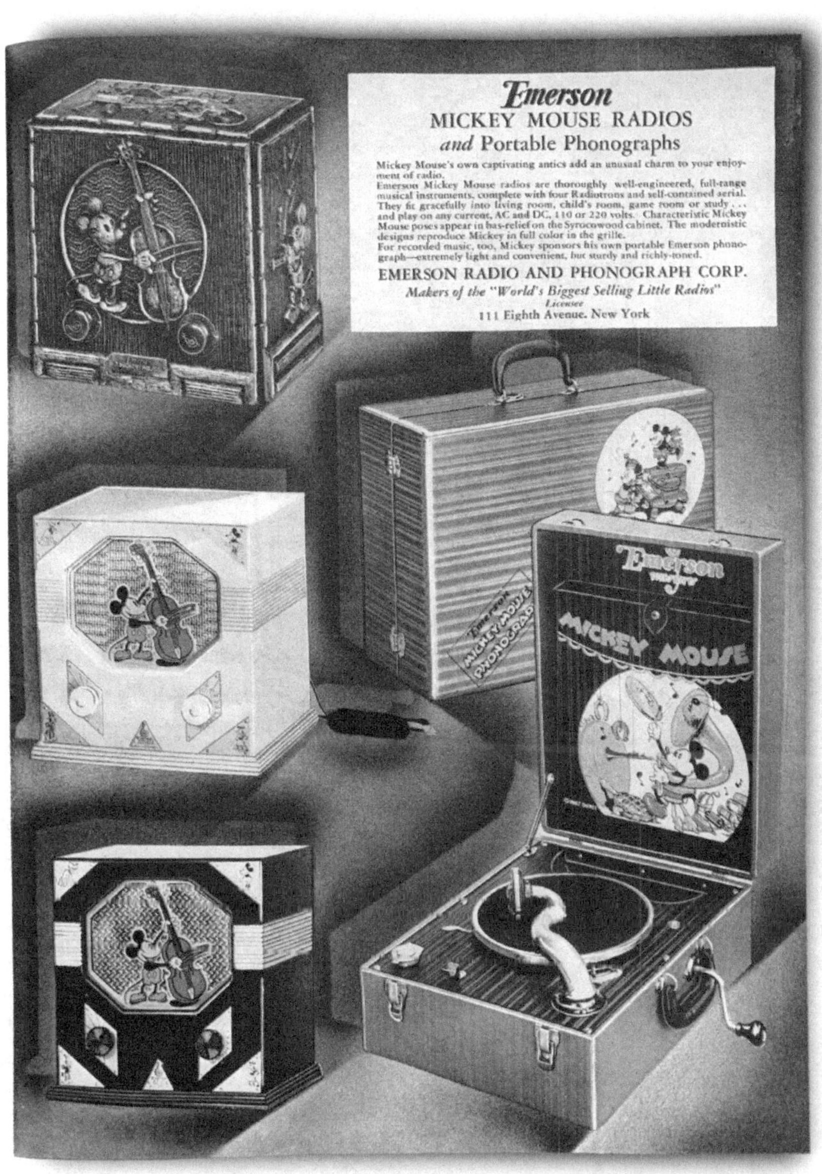

Emerson Radio and Phonograph Corp.
"Makers of the 'World's Biggest Selling Little Radios'"
1934 Mickey Mouse Merchandise Catalog

Mickey Mouse Play Houses
O. B. Andrews Co.
1934 Mickey Mouse Merchandise Catalog

RUBBER TOYS

Here's real appeal in Walt Disney Character rubber toys that parents and children love. Sunruco's skillful craftsmanship faithfully reproduces the animation and mold-detail of Mickey Mouse, Pluto, and Donald Duck in "fun-to-play-with" rubber toys. All are washable and especially processed to reduce dirt absorption.

#11013	Mickey Mouse "Squeeze" Doll
#12019	Mickey Mouse Aeroplane
#12018	Donald Duck Roadster
#12020	Mickey Mouse Tractor
#12017	Mickey Mouse Fire Truck

THE SUN RUBBER COMPANY
BARBERTON, OHIO

77

Rubber Toys
The Sun Rubber Company
1947 - 1948 Walt Disney Character Merchandise Catalog

WEATHER FORECASTER

Midget-size weather bureau for home use that's right from Disneyland with Donald Duck and Mickey Mouse in a real Disney house. Indicates weather changes from 8 to 24 hours in advance. Balmy days ahead when Mickey Mouse is out—Beware of rain when Donald Duck's about.

Walt Disney Character Weatherman to retail at $1.00

THE WEATHERMAN

430 NORTH MICHIGAN AVE., CHICAGO, 11, ILLINOIS

82

Weather Forecaster
The Weatherman
1947 - 1948 Walt Disney Character Merchandise Catalog

CHILDREN'S CAMERA

Walt Disney's Donald Duck and His Nephews are engraved right on the sturdy plastic (ethyl cellulose) case of the Donald Duck Camera that's a real camera — not a toy. Sales-pulling features are optically ground and polished Meniscus lenses, accurate eye level finder, and instantaneous shutter. Standard 127 film takes 12 pictures. Approved by Parents' Magazine.

Donald Duck Camera to retail at $1.98

HERBERT GEORGE CO.
311 NORTH DESPLAINES STREET, CHICAGO, 6, ILL;

35

Donald Duck Children's Camera
Herbert George Co.
1947 - 1948 Walt Disney Character Merchandise Catalog

Mickey & Minnie Mouse Save the Day!

With no arrow appearing on the seconds wheel and numerals 5 and 7 appearing opposite the knees, this 1933 Mickey Mouse "Long Stem" pocket watch is the very first model ever produced.
Author's Collection

It's interesting to consider that in 1933, during the unrelenting grip of the Great Depression, Mickey Mouse was taking the world by storm, and Kay Kamen was to fire up what would become a well-oiled Disney merchandise machine, opening an office in New York with a staff of 20 so as to begin cutting more licensing deals. However, while Walt, Roy, and Kay were growing sales at a fast pace, many other companies were suffering, one of which was the world-famous Ingersoll-Waterbury Watch Company. Though founded in 1892 and well known for "The Watch That Made the Dollar Famous", by 1933 sales had diminished to the point where the company had been forced to enter bankruptcy protection as a means to save its few remaining assets.

Being the innovator he was, Kamen sensed a potentially very lucrative opportunity, and he approached the beleaguered Ingersoll-Waterbury company with the idea of creating two special timepieces, a wristwatch and a pocket watch, both of which would feature Mickey Mouse on the face, with his yellow-gloved hands pointing to the time. Kay's intuition proved to be correct, as the wristwatch was an instant hit when introduced at the 1933 Chicago World's Fair at a price of only $1.50, nearly half that of the Ingersoll Mite, the watch upon which the Mickey Mouse model was based. Soon after, the wristwatch was introduced for sale at Macy's in New York, *where it sold 11,000 units in only one day...during the depression!* Bolstered by Mickey's growing worldwide fame, the time pieces continued to be popular, selling over 2½ million units over the next two years. In turn, the ensuing revenue allowed The Ingersoll-Waterbury Watch Company to avoid bankruptcy and instead expand its payroll during the heart of the depression from 200 employees to over 3,000 in the span of only a few weeks.

With an arrow now appearing on the seconds wheel and smaller numerals 5 and 7 appearing below the knees, this Mickey Mouse pocket watch was produced beginning six months after the very first model.

Mickey & Minnie Mouse Save the Day...Again!

1934 Lionel Mickey Mouse Handcar
Author's Collection

After the phenomenal success of Disney's partnership with the Ingersoll-Waterbury Watch Company, Kay Kamen recognized a similar opportunity with the Lionel Manufacturing Company, a beloved American toy manufacturer that was also facing hard times due to the depression.

In 1900, a young Joshua Lionel Cowen founded the Lionel Manufacturing Company with the goal of making miniature trains for use as a means to attract attention to retailers' storefront windows. However, store owners quickly discovered that customers weren't coming into their stores to buy what was on display in their windows, but instead they wanted to place an order for the miniature Lionel trains! Before he knew it, Mr. Cowen was selling toy trains and their detailed accessories to parents of children all across the country, and by 1928 the Lionel Company had become the leading manufacturer of toy trains in America, as well as overseas.

Unfortunately, the Great Depression of 1929 brought sales to a halt, as few families had the money available to buy such luxury items as toy trains. New locomotives, rolling stock, and layout pieces were produced in an attempt to drive sales, and even non-train items, such as a toy stove, were introduced so as to cater to girls and their mothers, but times were too difficult, and by May of 1934 The Lionel Company had gone into receivership and was facing bankruptcy.

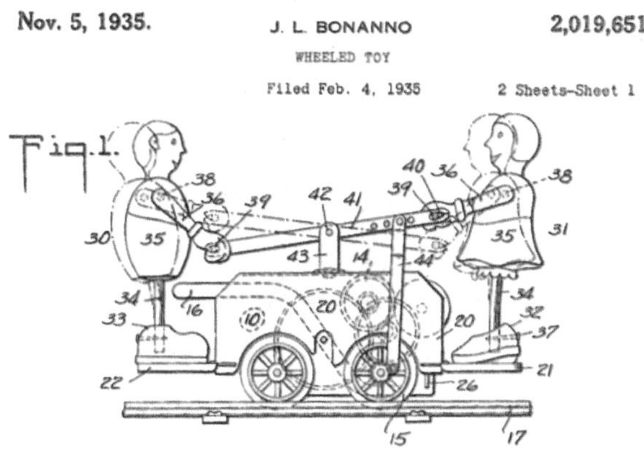

Seeing an opportunity for another deal like that he struck with the Ingersoll-Waterbury Watch Company, Kamen approached The Lionel Company in July of 1934 and suggested they work together to produce a new Lionel toy, a Mickey and Minnie Mouse Hand Car. Soon, a deal was signed and production began. Priced at only $1.00, families could again afford to buy a Lionel toy, one that included a wind-up hand car in red or green, a circular O-gauge track, and two of the most famous characters in the world at the controls, Mickey and Minnie Mouse. The toy was an instant and wildly popular hit, more so than the Mickey Mouse watches, selling one million units in about a year's time, thus saving The Lionel Company from bankruptcy and allowing it to continue down the tracks to create treasured memories for millions of families across America and around the world.

THE $300 "MYSTERY MAN"

Children's Writing Tablet
The Very First Disney Merchandise Item
Tablet Photo © Edward Bergen Collection

In the world of Disney merchandise, there exists a great mystery, one which to this day, even after considerable research, has never been solved...*Who was the man who approached Walt in a New York hotel lobby in 1929 and offered him $300 for the rights to put Mickey Mouse on the cover of a children's writing tablet?*

At one point, it was believed the mystery man was an employee of either the Powers Paper Co., which manufactured writing tablets and composition books for use by school children, or the American Lithographic Company, which, as you can imagine, created lithographic artwork. In looking into this mystery, I reached out to the Disney Consumer Products Archives division, who informed me that recent research into Disney's earliest merchandise projects casts doubts on the likelihood of the man being employed by either company.

Now, Disney knows their stuff, but my supposition, *with only very little circumstantial evidence to support it*, is that Occam's Razor applies here, and that the $300 mystery man did, indeed, work for the Powers Paper Company. Consider the following points:

- In 1929, Manhattan was considered to be *the* center of global merchandise licensing and distribution, with the International Toy Center, a complex of buildings located in the Flatiron District, being a hub for offices run by toy manufacturers and distributors.

- The Powers Paper Co., which was founded in 1857 and had been manufacturing paper products for 72 years by 1929, had its headquarters in Springfield, MA, but also had an office located at 200 Fifth Avenue in New York, which is the address for the International Toy Center complex. It would have been relatively easy and convenient for a representative of the Powers Paper Co., upon hearing Walt was in town, to make his way over to Walt's hotel and pitch the idea for the children's tablet.

- Walt and Roy created a new division of their company, Walt Disney Enterprises, on December 16, 1929 to manage and license Disney merchandise.

- The first Disney merchandise product, the children's writing tablet, was produced the following year, in 1930, as evidenced by the "© 1930 - Walter E. Disney" imprint on it's cover.

- The Powers Paper Co. obtained an *official* license to manufacture Mickey Mouse related writing tablets and composition books of different designs beginning in 1931, and this license ran until 1940. The Powers Paper Co. *may* have begun manufacturing the initial tablets in 1930 under the informal $300 handshake deal while negotiating the more formal 1931 agreement.

- All of the tablets manufactured by the Powers Paper Co. had an artistic style which differed noticeably from the first children's tablets produced...*except for one tablet*, and this could be a very important clue to the mystery!

- In Kay Kamen's 1934 Mickey Mouse Merchandise catalog, the Powers Paper Co. had a two page spread showcasing its collection of different writing tablets and composition books for school children. All of the tablets and books displayed had a similar design, *except for one*, which appeared in the upper left hand corner of the two page spread. This one tablet's design and artistic style differs noticeably from the rest of the Powers Paper Co. tablets and instead *matches more closely the artistic style of the first tablets produced under the $300 handshake deal.* Of note are the similarities in the graphic elements of the globe, as well as a geometric shape, in this case a large rectangle drawn in the image background, which is an artistic component that was used with the initial tablet designs, but not with any of the later Powers Paper Co. designs.

Of course, if we could see the lower left hand corner of the tablet appearing in the Kay Kamen catalog, we might find the same "© 1930 - Walter E. Disney" imprint we find on the initial tablets, and this would possibly solve this riddle, but as fate would have it, this nearly 100 year-old image holds fast to the mystery!

Chapter Five

Walt's Love of Trains

Walt Disney's Carolwood Pacific Railroad

Walt with his Lilly Belle and the Carolwood Pacific R. R.

Photo credit: Roger Broggie
Photo used with permission from The Broggie Family Trust

The following is an article written by Roger Broggie, the first Disney Imagineer, for the very first issue of *The Miniature Locomotive* magazine, which was printed in May of 1952. It is reprinted here with the permission of Roger Broggie's son, Michael Broggie.

THE CAROLWOOD PACIFIC RAILROAD, "The Fair Weather Route", is laid out on the side of a canyon on a quiet street in Beverly Hills, near the Pacific Ocean, in Southern California. It is owned and operated for pleasure, by Walt Disney, creator of Mickey Mouse, Donald Duck and other motion picture fairyland characters. Walt started his railroad career as a young "news butch" on the Missouri, Kansas and Texas R. R. and the

Missouri Pacific R. R., running out of Kansas City near where he was born. He has finally climbed the ladder of success, with an interlude of motion picture producing, to become President of this complete railroad, which although small in scale, is nevertheless "just like the big ones."

The train consists of a 1/8 scale miniature of a Central Pacific locomotive, six gondolas, two freight cars, two cattle cars and one caboose - all rolling stock is of the 1872-1880 period, running on 2600 feet of 7-1/4" gauge track laid out in a scenic pattern of trestles and tunnels along the edge of a canyon wall.

Walt's first experience with model railroading came with the construction of a Lionel train for a young nephew's Christmas present. He found this project a relaxation from his many duties as head of his studio. Therefore, he continued the hobby by assembling several locomotives and car kits in HO gauge and started an elaborate layout of an HO pike. But about this time, he had his first experience with live steam at Dick Jackson's one inch scale railroad in Beverly Hills. After an afternoon of running this train, the HO gauge pike was forgotten and a real LIVE STEAMER was born. He inspected and operated trains on several railroads before choosing 1-1/2" scale, 7-1/4" gauge as being the most suitable for his own layout. He liked the old time diamond stack locomotives of the 1880's for appearance and chose to follow a prototype typical of California. It was No. 173 of the Central Pacific R. R. built in Sacramento, California, in 1872, the first of ten similar locomotives built entirely on the Pacific Coast. Prior to this time, locomotives were manufactured in the East and either shipped to the West Coast by boat around the Horn or were shipped by rail after the transcontinental railroads were completed.

The Central Pacific No. 173

When Walt first contemplated building a steam model, he was surprised to find several among his employees that had experience with steam locomotives, both in full size and miniature. Among them are Ward Kimball, a top animator at the studio and owner of the Grizzly Flats R. R., a full size narrow gauge railroad, in his back yard in San Gabriel; Ollie Johnston, also an animator and owner of a 1" scale Pacific type steam locomotive and outdoor railroad, "The La Canada Valley Line"; Ed Sargeant, a mechanical draftsman at the studio with years of experience in miniature steam locomotive building.

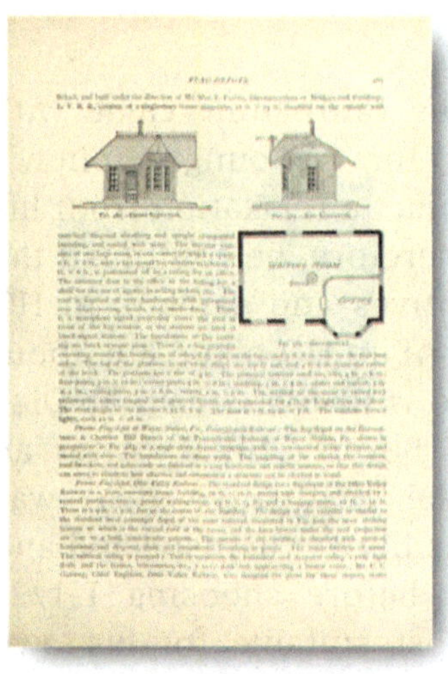

Books and photographs of early American railroads were furnished by Ward Kimball, Jerry Best of Warner Bros. Sound Dept. and a live steam enthusiast for many years, and Dick Jackson, Dean of all steam miniature railroaders of Southern California. Libraries and book dealers around the country were also combed for books. From this accumulation of data and a few blueprints from Southern Pacific R. R. files, working drawings for the Miniature No. 173 were started by Ed Sargeant in September, 1948. Patterns were also made in the studio prop shop by Ray Fox and George Bauer. Castings and fittings were made in the machine shop by Roger Broggie, Gene Foster, William Gillis and Dick Van Every.

Walt Disney came into the shop and learned to operate all the machine tools by making some of the parts himself. He made the whistle, flagstands and hand rails on the lathe. He learned sheet metal work by laying out and fabricating the headlamp and smoke stack. Then made numerous parts in the milling machine and learned to silver solder and braze on many small fittings. He now has a complete wood and metal workshop at his home.

The studio machine shop is regularly employed in maintenance work on cameras and other photographic equipment used to place the work of studio artists on theatre screens. Working on a part time basis, the shop built the locomotive and tender in time to steam up on December 24, 1949. A 300 foot test loop was laid on one of the Sound Stages and used for test runs until the outdoor track was laid. The locomotive was completed and cars made in 1950. The gondolas were made of cast aluminum by the shop.

Walt made the two box cars and cattle cars of wood in the studio prop shop, learning to operate all the woodworking machinery by doing so. He also made the caboose which is complete with running lights, bunks, clothes lockers, magazine rack with miniature newspapers, desk lamp, wash stand and a pot-bellied stove.

All the cars are mounted on arch bar trucks and are made up just as the original trucks were built. In fact, it got to be quite a saying around the shop that everything was "just like the big ones." We found that in following the practice of making everything just as it was made in the period of 1880-1900, gave the same kinds of trouble to us that the same equipment gave its owners in full size in the early days. Particularly this was true of arch bar trucks which are today barred on American railroads by the I.C.C. as being unsafe. We found them to be very rigid and liable to jump the track at any time. One reason for this was that as none of us in the shop had experience in railroad work before, we tended to make all fits too close, as we were used to machining parts for motion picture cameras and film equipment which generally have close tolerances. We did cure the tendency of track jumping in these trucks by making the side bearing plates free of the cars by about 1/8" on each side and making the center bearing loose in the center plate.

We approached the problem of laying the outdoor railway first as is done in full size practice but abandoned it for, what we termed the "Lionel Method" as being more practical. The layout was first plotted on paper at 1" - 20' scale. Full size masonite templates were made in 10' lengths in tangent and in radii from 45' to 60' in 5' steps and 100' radius, two templates of each required. The templates were laid on the ground, starting from the crossover point, and a record was made of the lengths of tangent and curved sections required to make the track go where the paper layout indicated. We tried to keep full 10' sections wherever possible since the dural rail comes in 10' lengths. The rail was rolled to the required radii in a set of motor driven rollers shaped to fit the rail contour. Then it was spiked to redwood ties in jigs. Ties were of scale section and length and rabbited for rail seating. They were also spaced in scale to full size practice. We dipped the rail spikes in a resin coating to make them hold tightly in the redwood ties and found it helped a lot. The rail was laid in all sections with a 3" offset and the track was bolted together in place on top of 2" crushed rock ballast. Ballast was added between the ties and tamped into place by a Mexican section gang who had had experience on the Southern Pacific R. R. laying track.

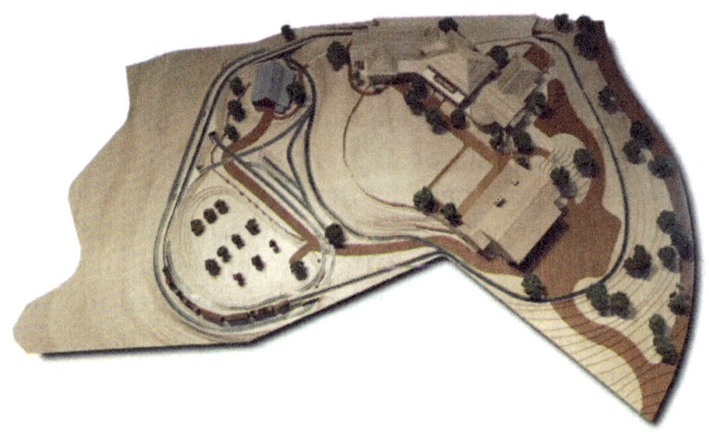

Layout of the Carolwood Pacific Railroad
As displayed at the Walt Disney Family Museum

The first part of the railroad was laid in December, 1950, and consisted of a complete loop with a figure 8 inside, one passing track and one siding. It required eleven switches and one crossover to join all these sections of track and totaled

1200 feet. The balance of track, laid in May, 1951, is one long loop of 1400 feet which climbs from the lower loop with two connecting curved sections of track having 3 per cent grades. This upper loop crosses a 65' long trestle which is 9' above the track it passes over and runs through a 90' long tunnel. It also crosses three other short overpasses and a 20' long trestle that is 3' high.

All this combination of track, bridges and tunnel were necessary because of the contour of the land and to enable the train to run in either direction over any part of the track. This gives a total ride of over 5,000 feet without going over the same track in the same direction twice.

Switches were laid out to have tunnels at tangent sections of track and are right and left hand turnouts using a No. 6 frog. Guard rails and switch points were made from the dural rail, frogs were of cast aluminum. The switches were nailed up on ties that were first nailed down to diagonal stringers. The switch stands are a combination of hand and electrical operation. Automatic controls are also installed in the track. Contacts in the rail make it impossible to trail an open switch and a control in the tender enables the driver to select either to turnout or keep on the main line when approaching from the point side. All these controls on the track enable a person when alone to run over the complete system in any direction without getting off the train to throw switches and without danger of derailing at open switches.

A CTC board is mounted in a dispatcher's office which is part of the red barn workshop in the center of the railroad area. From this control board any of the eleven railroad switches can be thrown, enabling a dispatcher to send a train over any route he selects.

The complete electrical system, which was designed by Lee Adams of the studio electrical department, was based on the principle of safety and convenience of train operation. Most of the train operators are friends of Walt Disney. A lot of them are celebrities of motion picture, radio and television fields, who know very little of the intricacies of railroad operation; the CTC system and safety contacts were installed so that anyone could be shown the throttle and reverse lever and sent on their way around the track without fear of having them go through open switches.

A second locomotive is being constructed at this time. It is a 4-6-0 or ten wheeler based on the same period as the No. 173. In fact, the pattern and drawings of the No. 173 are being used on this second locomotive. The changes being in the frame length and rods. This locomotive will be used for freight hauling and a set of passenger cars and mail cars will be built later to go with No. 173. A third locomotive and train is planned for the future, possibly a more modern locomotive. So with three trains running on the track, a CTC system becomes necessary to control the running of the trains to avoid wrecks, which again is the reason for everything being "just like the big ones."

RESTORING WALT'S LILLY BELLE

"Yes, in one way or another, I have always loved trains."

- Walt Disney

Walt Disney loved trains nearly his entire life. From his job as a News Butch on the Missouri Pacific railroad as a 15 year-old in Kansas City to the trains he made sure encircle Disney theme parks around the world, Walt was captivated by these grand machines and everything about them. It is because of this passion that he designed and built, along with Roger E. Broggie, his own working 1/8 scale steam train, which he ran on a half-mile track in the backyard of his Holmby Hills, California home on Carolwood Drive. A line he called the *Carolwood Pacific Railroad.*

Pulling the rolling stock of the *Carolwood Pacific* was the Lilly Belle, a locomotive that Walt modeled after the Central Pacific No. 173, an 1872 steam locomotive with a design he felt captured the historical essence of railroading.

As the demands upon Walt's time grew with the planning, designing, and construction of Disneyland, he found he had less and less time available to run his *Carolwood Pacific.* As a result, his beloved Lilly Belle steam engine was put into storage, moving to different locations before finally finding a home on display in Disneyland's Main Street Railroad Station, where it remained into the 1990s. On a couple of occasions through the years, the engine and rolling stock were crated and shipped for display at notable events, including at the Nixon Library, the Reagan Library, and the California State Railroad Museum. Unfortunately, the rigors of time took its toll on the Lilly Belle, resulting in minor damage, with the paint becoming scuffed, parts being bent, pieces having broken, and others missing entirely.

In 2002, Michael Campbell, then President of the Carolwood Pacific Historical Society, recognized that the Lilly Belle needed not only restoration, but also preservation, as it had become a highly revered and priceless artifact of Disney history. That year, Campbell created an exhibition that celebrated Walt's love of railroading at the California State Railroad Museum. This afforded him the opportunity to closely inspect the Lilly Belle and her tender, which served as the centerpiece of the show. He was concerned to see the deteriorating condition of the Lilly Belle: most notably, the hinged cab roof - hand-made by Walt - had split in two.

Years later, Diane Disney Miller and her son, Walter Elias Disney Miller, decided to create a museum that would explore and celebrate Walt Disney's remarkable life and achievements. They asked Michael to oversee all of the railroad-related exhibits in this state-of-the-art museum. Naturally, the Lilly Belle would have an honored place among the various displays. With the museum scheduled to open in October of 2009, Michael realized the timing would be perfect to have Walt's restored Lilly Belle included in the grand opening ceremonies of the museum. With this in mind, he proposed a careful restoration of the Lilly Belle.

There were two distinct schools of thought regarding the restoration effort...should the team focus on restoration or preservation? The preservationists working for the Walt

Disney Family Museum felt that the damage that had occurred subsequent to Walt's passing was part of the story of the Lilly Belle and should be stabilized and preserved. The other approach, advocated by Michael, was that Walt poured great attention into constructing the Lilly Belle, and he was careful to have the engine beautifully presented whenever it appeared in photos or on film. Diane respected both viewpoints and was considering both until Michael shared with her a piece of information that clarified her father's intent. Walt wrote an article, entitled "I have always loved trains", for the October 1965 issue of "Railroad Magazine". The last paragraph of the article includes this statement by Walt: *'What happened to the Carolwood Pacific train? I still have it. I'm going to get it repainted and displayed in a glass case at the Disneyland and Santa Fe station.'* This comment proved to Diane that her father recognized the need to restore the Lilly Belle during his lifetime. Campbell later remarked:

"After all, out of all the things Walt Disney created, he only named one after his wife, Lillian Disney. It's hard to imagine that he would want it put on display for the world to see with obvious problems."

Diane asked Michael to work with the Museum staff to carefully restore the Lilly Belle. This included fixing a broken window and rods, restoring bent fenders, repairing the cab roof, and undoing damage caused by some large, ugly screws that had been used to secure the roof to the rest of the cab. The cab and other cosmetic restorations were performed by the Museum's Conservationist, Tonja Morris. Tonja's work was stunning, as she masterfully erased all evidence of damage to the cab.

For the mechanical details, Michael contacted Sean Bautista, whom he knew shared not only Walt's love of trains, but also his attention to detail. Sean said he'd be more than honored to help in the restoration effort, so Michael introduced him to Diane Disney Miller, Ron Miller, and the Disney curators who would be overseeing the project.

Working from a set of original drawings, Sean cautiously and methodically undertook the restoration effort, carefully coaxing bends from the fenders, refurbishing the hoses to the Tender, realigning the pilot truck, and restoring the Smokebox. Throughout this, he would at times be struck by the significance of the project he had been entrusted with...

Walt Disney's Lilly Belle Locomotive
On display at the Walt Disney Family Museum in San Francisco

"There were a number of times in which I'd sit back in my chair, pinch myself, and realize that I was actually working on Walt's personal locomotive, the Lilly Belle, and holding in my hands the very same pieces that he himself had held so many years before."

Though a great deal of time had passed, in every piece he worked on Sean could clearly see the evidence of Walt's handiwork, as well as that of the Imagineers who helped him build the Lilly Belle.

"You'd be surprised how each Imagineer has their own unique and distinct style, be it Walt, Bob Gurr, Roger Broggie, or whomever. Just as different classical painters have their own unique brush strokes, each Imagineer who helped build

Disneyland and the Disneyland Railroad has their own unique signature of craftsmanship, and I can study a Disney locomotive and easily discern the handiwork of those Imagineers who helped create and build it."

After months of careful work, Walt's engine was restored to the time of when he was at the throttle, and on October 1, 2009, his daughter, Diane, dedicated the new Walt Disney Family Museum in San Francisco with the Lilly Belle now preserved and on display for generations of Disney fans and guests to enjoy.

My thanks to Sean Bautista, Michael Campbell, and Michael and Sharon Broggie for their generous contributions to this article.

THE RESTORATION OF THE LILLY BELLE PRESIDENTIAL CAR

The following article was graciously contributed by Steve DeGaetano, author of the outstanding book "*Welcome Aboard the Disneyland Railroad! - The Complete History in Words and Pictures - Collector's Edition*"

In November of 1996, the *Lilly Belle* presidential car of the Disneyland Railroad was pulled off-line and put into rehab to restore and improve both the exterior and interior of the car, bringing it up to a "presidential' level. After this rehab, the car soldiered on several more years. But with every passing year, a new problem was festering under the surface: dry rot.

The car's wooden construction had survived decades of use, but now the effects of moisture were beginning to take their toll. The exterior wood was becoming brittle and fragile, and in the late 1990s the car was once again removed from the line.

Unfortunately, those in charge of the Park were not too keen on spending a literal trainload of money to restore a car that few guests would ever experience. Even some pragmatic roundhouse cast members considered the car "dead weight" that added unnecessary tonnage to their trains, continuing to tax their already maxed out smaller scale locomotives. And so, once again, the stately observation car of the Disneyland Railroad was quietly stored away, out of sight, in the back of the roundhouse. There she remained, partially dismantled and windows boarded up, for several years, seemingly forgotten.

Various proposals by cast members to work on the car themselves came and went, and were sometimes the cause of inter-union disputes. Who should rebuild the car? The roundhouse crew, who primarily belonged to boiler or machinist unions, or Disney's union carpenters? All the while, the car continued to deteriorate, with one cast member commenting that the wood siding was so depleted in some areas that he could easily "put a finger" through it. Many guests may not have missed the car, but there were a significant number of knowledgeable fans who wondered about the beloved car that had so much history. Frequently, Disney-oriented Internet message boards had threads that asked, "What's the condition of the *Lilly Belle*?" or "Where's the *Lilly Belle*?" Clearly, folks missed her.

Everything changed in late April 2005. The Disneyland Resort had a new president in Matt Ouimet, who understood far more than his predecessors about the importance of "show" and "plussing" attractions. Ouimet was at the Park participating in a ceremony for Disney Legend and animator Ollie Johnston on May 12, 2005. At the conclusion of the ceremony, Ouimet was on his way back to the Team Disney Anaheim building, but made a detour to the roundhouse. He strolled up to the cast members in the roundhouse, and - according to one cast member there that day - made a simple, straightforward request: "I want to see the *Lilly Belle*."

Several additional inspections followed. Folks knew things were getting serious when Jeff Kaye, a representative of Retlaw, was asked to provide photographs of the car's interior so that an accurate reconstruction could take place.

Things happened rather fast after that. In the early summer, while the Disneyland roundhouse was preparing the debut of their newest locomotive, *Ward Kimball*, plans were underway to have the *Lilly Belle* sent off-site for a complete rebuild.

In August, a contract had been signed with Tim Lagaly of R. B. Builders, located in Camarillo, California, and the lovely presidential car was trucked to the facility to begin her five month rebuild. Lagaly won the contract for a very good reason: he had previous experience restoring the original "combine" of the train. Because of his hands-on experience, Lagaly knew all about the construction techniques used on the Disney cars.

The September 9, 2005 issue of the Disneyland Line contained an article on the progress, noting that the work "encompasses new siding and roof, refurbished mechanical equipment, and new exterior paint and signage. Inside, new carpet and refinished paneling and furniture will complete the restoration."

The car was returned to Disneyland the first week of December 2005, where work began to restore her interior. There were a few alterations to the car. The six rooftop vents seen in earlier photos were removed completely, as they had allowed water to enter and do damage to the roof. Brand new cast-brass nameplates, similar to the originals, were installed on the doors. A brand-new drumhead was created with the car's name. The black marker lamps, hand-made by Roger Broggie Jr., were found to be made of brass, so the paint was simply stripped and the brass polished up to make for beautiful "jewelry" on the car.

On the inside, the mirror on the left wall was removed. The original seats were reupholstered. New Disney family pictures were installed, as well as other knick-knacks, such as books Walt might have enjoyed and crystal sets. (all securely glued down to prevent theft!) On the back wall, authentic railroad lamps with the letters "GWR" (Great Western Railway) were installed. The brass-platted fans were made operable. Imagineer Kim Irvine, who once again oversaw the re-decoration of the car, wished to create a stronger connection with the car's namesake, Lillian Disney, so she found an old smoking jacket, very similar to the one Lillian used to wear, and hung it in the car. (This jacket is often mistakenly said to actually be Lillian's or even Walt's smoking jacket by some tour guides and conductors.)

On the floor, brand new carpet was installed. This led to more information that is often passed on by tour guides and conductors, who sometimes tell guests that the carpet is the last remaining piece of the original *Lilly Belle* carpet, and that it's the same carpet used in Walt's firehouse apartment. The carpet *is* the same as that used in the apartment, but the carpet there is brand new, too - that carpet was replaced years ago because of water damage, and the same roll provided for use in the *Lilly Belle.*

Another frequently repeated misconception is that the wood on the clerestory ceiling is inlaid with a different color wood, to create a unique design. The clerestory design is merely stenciled on with lighter colored paint. The fact that so many people mistake it for inlaid wood is testament to the skill of the Disneyland painters.

A month later, the car passed her roundhouse inspection and was attached to the rear of the Holiday Blue train an hour before Park closing on January 10, 2006, pulled by the *Ward Kimball.* Very few people were on hand to see her that late in the evening. The next day, she debuted in broad daylight, merely waiting to pass her DOSH inspections before she could begin accepting passengers. She initially made only dry runs, without passengers, while the conductors began their special training for the car. Soon, however, the elegant car would be open for passengers.

On the morning of February 15, 2006, prior to the Park opening, Matt Ouimet - whose concern about the *Lilly Belle's* condition nine months earlier had led to her renovation - would formally welcome the car back to Disneyland in grand style. The day was to be a two-fer - The *Ward Kimball* steam locomotive would also be dedicated. I (Steve DeGaetano) was invited to attend the ceremony by Tim O'Day, former head of Disneyland PR. I arrived early with Matt Walker, and we met O'Day near the roundhouse. We made our way to the platform at Frontierland Station, and I was introduced to Matt Ouimet. We shook hands, and Ouimet told me he had stayed up the night before reading my book on the Disneyland Railroad, so he would know what technical terms to use in his prepared remarks.

After Disneyland Ambassador Andrae Rivas introduced the event, the Ward Kimball whistled into the station, pulling a single Holiday Green car filled with Steam Train cast members.

Attached to the rear of that car was the *Lilly Belle.* Matt Ouimet spoke of Walt Disney's passion for trains and how that influence is still felt on the Disneyland Railroad. Following Ward's son John Kimball's dedication of the *Ward Kimball*, the honored guests were invited aboard to tour the *Lilly Belle.*

Sadly, Walt Disney never got to see the *Lilly Belle* built, but he no doubt would have been very proud of the work Disneyland accomplished in transforming the Grand Canyon into the sumptuous car.

Today, over 60 years after the *Lilly Belle* first took to the rails, we can once again enjoy seeing her at the tail end of one of the trains. The car that many believed would never again see the light of day now delights young and old alike with her Victorian splendor and detailing. While not all of us may get to ride her, we can appreciate the elegance of the car, and revel in the history she represents. Long may the *Lilly Belle* ride the rails of the Disneyland Railroad!

Walt Joins the Southern California Live Steamers

Many of Walt's inspirations for the Disneyland Railroad and Main Street, U.S.A. came from his involvement with miniature "live steam" railroading. But while Walt had always had a love of trains since he was a child, his interest in miniature railroading would begin later in his life, during the late 1940s.

With the worldwide success of Mickey Mouse and his ground-breaking animated movies, *Snow White, Pinocchio,* and *Fantasia*, Walt was busier than ever as he managed his growing Disney Studios and a new slate of films during the early 1940s. Unbeknownst to him at the time, there was a new community of railfans dedicated to the world of miniature live steam railroading growing in the Southern California area, a world that Walt would ultimately find himself a part of whenever he stepped away from the daily rigors of his job.

On September 18, 1941, Dick Jackson and 34 charter members, including Disney animator Ward Kimball, Disney Studios draftsman Eddie Sargeant, and future Disney employee Dick Bagley met at the Sherman Oaks home of Mr. Bagley with the purpose of founding the new Southern California Live Steamers club, the first club of its kind in the state dedicated to the world of miniature "live steam" railroading. Soon, members began meeting regularly at 8:00 p.m. on the second Thursday of every month in the homes of various club members, and on one Sunday a month they and their families would gather in Mr. Jackson's backyard to run his 4-4-0 locomotive, the 900, and to ride his miniature steam train along his layout, the *Colorado Central*, which was one of the largest miniature railroads in the country.

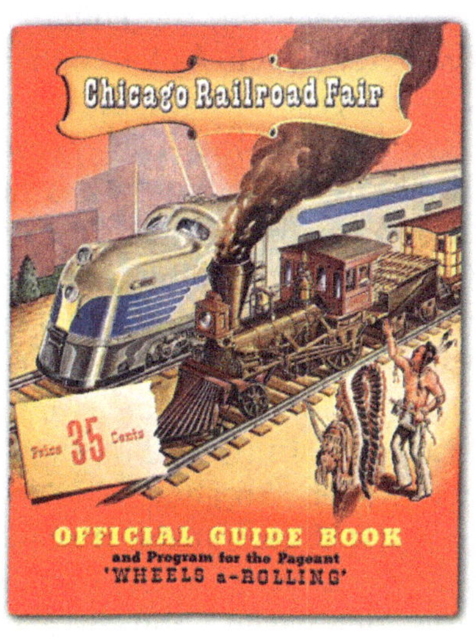

1948 Chicago Railroad Fair - Official Guide Book
Author's Collection

In August of 1948, Walt, along with Ward Kimball, had the opportunity to attend the Chicago Railroad Fair, a mile long exposition on the shores of Lake Michigan, which showcased 100 years of railroad progress. Immersed in all aspects of railroading for the duration of his visit, from historical locomotives to the newest "mammoth streamliners", Walt returned from the fair and told his wife, Lilly, "*That was the most fun I ever had in my life.*" Drawing inspiration from the fair, he was thrilled to see the possibility of combining his passion for railroading with his interest in miniatures, and as a result, he now set his sights on building his own miniature steam locomotive and railroad.

Shortly after they returned from the fair, Ward invited Walt to attend a "steam up" of his locomotive, the Emma Nevada, at his *Grizzly Flats Railroad*, which was located at his home in San Gabriel. Steam ups at Ward and Betty Kimball's place were festive affairs, and they were usually attended by club members, neighbors, friends, and even Hollywood stars and dignitaries, all in a party-like atmosphere as the large coal burning Emma Nevada chuffed its way back and forth past a depot and water tank along 900' of narrow-gauge track. It was here that Walt met Dick Jackson, the Founder of the Southern California Live Steamers, which had now been an active and growing club for seven years. With their shared interests in railroading and live steam, the two men became instant friends. Walt no doubt discussed with Dick his new interest in building a miniature railroad, and in turn Dick invited Walt to visit his Beverly Hills home to see his *Colorado Central* and to operate his miniature locomotive, the 900. Taking Dick up on his invitation, Walt was captivated by all aspects of the *Colorado Central*, and it only spurred his enthusiasm to build his own backyard railroad. In the fall of 1948, with the help of Disney Imagineers Roger Broggie, Eddie Sargeant, Ward Kimball, Dick Bagley and others at the Disney Studios machine shop, Walt began the construction of an intricately designed miniature locomotive, one based upon the classic design of the 1872 4-4-0 Central Pacific No. 173.

While work on his locomotive and the corresponding tender and rolling stock progressed, Walt knew he would need some land on which to run his new train, so in June of 1949 he purchased five acres of property in the Holmby Hills area of Los Angeles. Here, he would have the room he wanted to build a new home, as well as his new miniature railroad.

The precision machining and proper assembly of all the components for Walt's locomotive, tender, and rolling stock took some time, as the studio machine shop crew, which was normally creating and maintaining cameras and other photographic equipment for the production of Disney movies, was working on a part time basis on Walt's project, but on December 24, 1949 they steamed up the new locomotive for the very first time, taking it for a test run on 300' of track at one of the Disney sound stages. A little over five months later, on May 7, 1950, the beautiful *Lilly Belle* locomotive, named after Walt's wife, Lillian, made its official debut in the backyard of Walt and Lillian's new home and was soon pulling rolling stock and entertaining guests along 2,600' of 7-1/4" gauge track on a layout that Walt would call the *Carolwood Pacific*, named after the street on which he lived in the Holmby Hills neighborhood, Carolwood Drive.

The undercarriage of Walt's Lilly Belle engine, as it was being built at the Disney Studios machine shops. Of note is that Walt himself built the headlight and smokestack.

During the construction of the Lilly Belle steam engine and his *Carolwood Pacific*, Walt became a member of the Southern California Live Steamers club. It was in this club that he could step away from the pressures of creating such films as *Cinderella, Treasure Island,* and *Alice in Wonderland*, and instead relax and enjoy his passion for miniature railroading while socializing with fellow live steam enthusiasts, hearing about their different locomotives and layouts in development, and offering rides aboard his new *Carolwood Pacific.*

Walt joined the Southern California Live Steamers club in 1948, with his name first appearing in a 1950 membership booklet. The following image is a look at not only a set of very rare original booklets issued by the club, but also Walt's listing as it appears in the 1950 edition...

A collection of extremely rare 1948 - 1952
Southern California Live Steamers membership booklets
Author's Collection

Walt's listing reflects the Disney Studios at 2400 Alameda Avenue in Burbank...

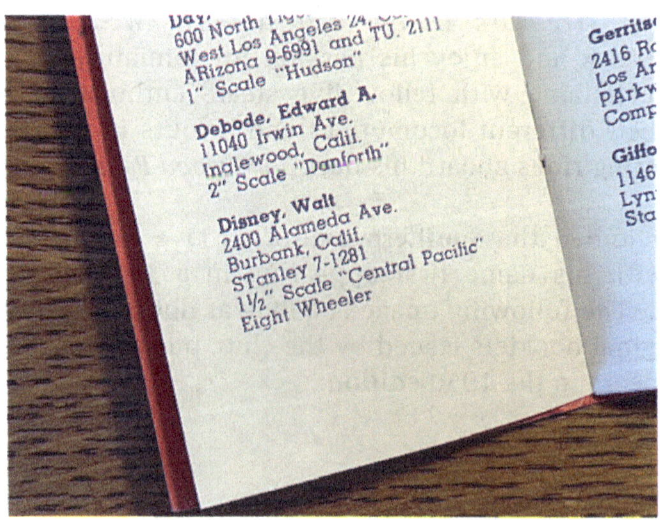

600 North
West Los Angeles 24,
ARizona 9-6991 and TU. 2111
1" Scale "Hudson"

Debode, Edward A.
11040 Irwin Ave.
Inglewood, Calif.
2" Scale "Danforth"

Disney, Walt
2400 Alameda Ave.
Burbank, Calif.
STanley 7-1281
1½" Scale "Central Pacific"
Eight Wheeler

In 1953, an accident occurred on the *Carolwood Pacific* in which the Lilly Belle ran off the tracks and a young girl received some minor burns on her legs from a jet of steam emitting from the locomotive. As a result of the accident, Walt put the Lilly Belle into storage and now turned his attention to an idea that had been percolating in his mind for quite some time: building a much larger railroad, one that would encircle a new theme park that he would call...Disneyland.

WALT DISNEY'S OLD TIME RAILROAD

The small ad Walt placed in "The Miniature Locomotive Magazine", which offered for sale copies of the plans he used to build his Lilly Belle locomotive. - Author's Collection

With the building of the *Carolwood Pacific*, members of the Southern California Live Steamers group, as well as other steam enthusiasts and the public in general, took note and were soon asking Walt to share details of his new locomotive so they too may build a steam engine like his new Lilly Belle. As part of the Lilly Belle's construction, Walt, Roger Broggie, and his team had acquired blueprints of the Central Pacific No. 173 from Southern Pacific and, through the work of Eddie Sargeant, converted these into 35 detailed drawings. Initially, Walt would send copies of these blueprints to interested parties, but as word got out and demand for the blueprints increased, he found he didn't have time to dedicate to this task, so he created *Walt Disney's Old Time Railroad* and hired Dick Bagley, the former President of the Southern California Live Steamers club, as well as co-editor and publisher of *The Miniature*

Locomotive Magazine, to manage and run this new small "business". In turn, Dick placed ads in *The Miniature Locomotive Magazine* for a catalog offering a "*Complete set of castings and drawings in 1-1/2" scale as used to build Walt Disney's own locomotive.*" With this, model train enthusiasts across the country could order their own parts and build a model steam locomotive just like Walt's.

The price of this catalog that Walt was selling at the height of his fame when his movies were making millions of dollars around the world?...35 cents!

PUBLISHING WALT'S LOVE OF MODEL RAILROADING

Walt during a little publicized trip to the Chingford Model Railroad in Ridgeway Park, London, July 12, 1952

During the mid-1950s through mid-1960s, there was a small number of railfan magazines which published a handful of articles about such things as Walt Disney's love of trains, the steam trains of Disneyland, and the personal "backyard" railroads of such Disney artists and Imagineers as Ollie Johnston, Dick Bagley, and Ward Kimball. Above, Walt is showing off the inaugural May - June, 1952 edition of *The Miniature Locomotive* magazine to new friends in London, England, which features a photo of Walt aboard his Lilly Belle steam engine on the front cover and an article inside written by Roger Broggie about Walt's *Carolwood Pacific Railroad* in the backyard of his Holmby Hills home.

Now over 75 years old, these obscure magazine articles are rarely, if ever, seen by Disney fans. However, the following article is a profile of Ward Kimball, who helped Walt design the steam engines of Disneyland, among many other contributions, and it appeared in the April, 1965 issue of *Railroad Magazine.*
- Reprint permission courtesy of White River Productions

Ward Kimball
Interesting Railfans No. 28

Ward Kimball and Walt Disney Aboard the Emma Nevada

The following is a profile of Ward Kimball, as it appeared in the April, 1965 issue of Railroad Magazine.

Ward Kimball is the most versatile railfan we have ever known. He invented a talking cricket, coached a chorus of singing crows, and plotted a trip to the moon - all in movie cartoons. He by-lined a book that is probably banned by every school and public library in the country. He is a railroad president and amateur astronomer. He collects vintage automobiles and other Americana, plays the trombone, and is a licensed airplane pilot.

Said Ralph J. Gleason, columnist for the San Francisco Chronicle: "Ward Kimball is a short, slight man with a face like an old-time vaudeville comic. He slaves for the big money in the Disney factories in Lotusland and for ten years or so, in between building a railroad in his back yard, he has operated a Dixieland band."

Another columnist, Jim Davis, wrote in The Parsons (Kan.) Sun: "When Ward Kimball was a five-year old, he played here in the junk locomotives of a Katy Railroad graveyard. As a result, he became a railroad buff who now has three antique Baldwin locomotives in his back yard. He also grew up to be a movie director, band leader, and author."

Two important events happened in 1914: (a) Ward Kimball was born at Minneapolis on March 14th and (b) an Austrian archduke was assassinated June 28th. The world has not been the same ever since.

On approximately the same date as the Battle of St. Mihiel in France, the subject of this sketch, then four years old, touched a locomotive for the first time, the engine being a 4-4-0 and the place being the Frisco depot at Parsons. "Frequent trips to the Parsons waterworks," Ward recalls, "where the Katy Flyer used to roar around the curve with much smoke and whistling, also were a contributing factor to my early love of railroads."

Later, back in Minneapolis and aged seven, he started on a collecting spree that he'll probably never outgrow: Cigar bands, streetcar transfers, and tin toy trolleys. (What was there about Minneapolis that gave residents the trolley bug? Frank P. Donovan, No 19 in our *Interesting Railfans* series, chartered a Minneapolis trolley for his wedding party and wrote transit articles for *Railroad Magazine*.)

Luckily, Ward had other interests. He took to drawing steam locomotives and he fell for a correspondence course in cartooning. In due time he enrolled at Stanford U. but didn't care much for college. Someone has said that "College is the place where pebbles are polished and diamonds are dimmed." Ward avoided both possibilities by winning a scholarship to the Santa Barbara Art School, quitting Stanford, and studying art.

After two years of painting trees, barns, and nudes, the lad decided he was pretty good. He was then twenty. Taking his nerve into both hands, he asked Walt Disney for a job. Disney had recently opened a studio to make Mickey Mouse cartoons for the movies and he needed animators. He looked at Ward's stuff and said, "You start here tomorrow morning at nine."

Ward was elated. He was then the youngest animator on Disney's staff. An animator, in case you didn't know, is one of the artists who draw the sequence of pictures that, when photographed and flashed on a screen, make a cartoon *move.* After doing this work for some time and occasionally writing scripts, Ward was promoted to the job of designing and directing short movie cartoons. One of these, *Toot, Whistle, Plunk and Boom*, won an Academy Award. Today he is a top animation supervisor on the Disney totem pole.

"This wonderful world of cartoons and live action," says Ward, "has never seemed to me like hard work. I love it."

When Disney embarked on television programs, our No. 28 Railfan was put in charge of *Tomorrowland* segments, including the space travel series, one of which won a TV Emmy Award. And when that fabulous amusement resort known as Disneyland was being planned, Ward served as railroad technical advisor, seeing that everything on the Disneyland Railroad was as authentic as possible. For reference material, he used his large collection of old railbooks and files of *Railroad Magazine.*

"It thrilled me," he recalls, "to watch all this wonderful equipment come to life and made me feel rather important to be part of the planning."

In the late '30's, with the economic independence of a steady, well-paying job, he began building old-time railroad models in ¼" scale as a hobby. His layout was pre-1890. No kits - everything built from scratch. He put in week-ends tracking down equipment, measuring, and drawing.

In 1934 he began dating a personable young blonde named Betty Lawyer, a color consultant at Disney's, and he married her in '36. Ward spent many *daylight* hours of his honeymoon on detailed drawings of Virginia & Truckee equipment. (Betty must have *loved* that!) Today, in spite of all this, they have two daughters, Kelly, 25, and Chloe, 18, and a son John, 23, as well as a granddaughter.

Ward's Grizzly Flats Railroad

We asked Ward about the Grizzly Flats Railroad that operates on the three-acre "back-yard" of the Kimball home on a quiet, tree-lined street at 8910 Ardendale Avenue, San Gabriel, Calif. Apparently it all started with the news that the Southern Pacific's narrow-gage at Keeler, Calif., was going to burn up its antique coaches.

"Betty and I rushed up there," he says, "and found that they wanted only $50 for an old coach. So we bought one, with the idea of turning it into a railroad museum behind the house, and we picked up enough 35-pound rail to rest it on."

"My original idea for a railroad museum was expanded when I learned that the Nevada Central, another narrow-gage line, was planning to sell its old steam engines to Japan for scrap. I purchased one of them, the *Emma Nevada*, for a mere $400."

She was No. 2, a Mogul, the last motive power to run on the NC, her final job having been hauling flatcars with scrap rail to Battle Mount, Nev. Baldwin had built her in 1881, construction number 5575; cylinders 13 x 18", weight 44,000 pounds, drivers 41" in diameter, and wheelbase 17'1".

The freight bill for hauling her to Los Angeles in a gondola was $450. Before being unloaded, she was given a rigid inspection in the SP shops. They checked her injectors, lubricators, and 8" air pump, and set the pops at 100 pounds, instead of 135, for reasons of safety. A truck then moved her to the Kimball homestead.

More track had to be laid. Track-laying is not a one-man job. But Ward Kimball was foxy. He'd read in a Mark Twain book how Tom Sawyer was given the irksome task of whitewashing a long fence. Instead of doing the job himself, Tom convinced the boys of the neighborhood that they could have fun by helping him - and they fell for his "line." By volunteer help, the fence was whitewashed with very little muscular effort on Tom's part. What Ward Kimball did, conniving with Betty, was to throw periodic tracklaying barbecues to induce friends and neighbors to assist. It worked. Today, the Grizzly Flats boasts 950 feet of "main line," thanks partly to outsiders.

"In those days," Ward tells us, "San Gabriel was largely citrus-ranch country. Some of the neighboring farmers used to stand in front of our home and wonder what was going on back there. It must have been strange for them to watch puffing steam engines move back and forth behind the house, apparently with no place to go.

"Betty and I would invite them onto our property to enjoy what was going on. For many years the Grizzly Flats has been the scene of happy gatherings of railroad buffs, women's clubs, model fans, youth groups, school classes, and lovers of Americana in general.

Meanwhile, the 2-6-0 had to be put into operating condition. There were tedious weeks of cleaning and scraping with putty knives and caustic soda. Layers of old paint were removed from both engine and tender. When the original layer was reached, care was taken to measure all lettering and striping, and the quaint decorations were recorded on tracing paper, so as to duplicate the original exactly in the final painting.

The tender tank was sand-blasted to remove all rust, and was red-leaded. Everything cleaned on the loco also was given a protective coast of red lead. But a disheartening discovery was the finding of dry rot in the oak tender frame. This necessitated complete rebuilding of that frame, after the old one has been measured accurately. It was a long and painstaking job.

Then the well-pitted throttle valve had to be ground to insure a tight seat, and a new throttle with new packing was put into place. The broken reverse lever spring was replaced, new running boards were installed, and a new 5-foot pilot was built from old SP narrow-gage blueprints. Brass flag-holders, acorn trims, and grab railings were added.

One of the many volunteer helpers was Gerald M. Best (No. 16 in our *Interesting Railfans* series), who supplied a genuine old Baldwin oilburning headlight from a Carson & Colorado engine. Atop the sandbox was attached a quaint bronze American eagle in full flight. The old wooden cab required a maximum of bracing and refitting, a roof canvas was tacked into place, and ruby red windows etched with flowers were installed.

Next came the relatively easy paint job - three coats: engine and tender wheels vermillion, striped in gold leaf; pilot headlight domes deep carmine red, also trimmed with gold leaf; cylinders and steam chest deep green and vermillion with gold-leaf floral designs; cab olive green and Venetian red, and the undercarriage and valve motion black and red. Ward himself painted nostalgic pictures on the headlight.

The tender is black, trimmed with carmine, green, and orange, and lettered *Grizzly Flats R.R.* A bit of sentiment was added by glueing pin-up girls of the '90's above the windows inside the cab. Finally, the coach was finished in gaudy canary yellow with apple-green letter boards, maroon-trimmed windows, and gold filigree. What a riot of color!

But those jobs were little more than a beginning. Other equipment was acquired, structures were built. As Ward says: "Back-yard railroading is like painting the Brooklyn Bridge. You start working from one end to the other, and then you begin all over again."

Today, alone or in groups, visitors are welcomed to the Grizzly Flats Railroad. They ride the train, gape at the 1900-model windmill, gaze up admiringly at the 7,200-gallon water tower, and browse through the 1856 vintage wooden depot.

This depot, gaily painted red and orange, is authentic in every detail. Actually, Ward designed it for a Disney film (*So Dear to My Heart*) and later salvaged it from a set at the Disney studios. It now houses one of the nation's finest displays of railroadiana - buttons from passenger trainmen's uniforms, switch locks and keys, old dining-car menus, passes, tickets, posters, lanterns, watches, locomotive bells and headlights, and antique toy trains.

Aside from his railroad items, Ward has other Americana. For example: a wooden "gingerbread" doll house, made about 1890, and dolls dating back to the 1850's, and character toys from the 1920's representing celebrities of their day.

Down at the south end of the yard you can see the enginehouse, also built by ward with friends' help. Inside stand the *Emma Nevada*, that 20-ton coalburner, and coach No. 5, built in 1873, the SP's last narrow-gage passenger car and two sugar-plantation steam engines from Hawaii: the Chloe, which Ward acquired in 1948 and named for his younger daughter, and the Olomana (Big Noise), owned by "Jerry" Best. Guarding the grade crossing near the family garage is the Pennsy-type watchman's shanty of the 1870's, and beside the depot you can't miss the big, old hand-operated target-stub switch, a V&T relic.

Among other equipment is a 40-foot boxcar, a 40-foot side-door caboose from the old Pacific Coast Railway, and a 3-foot-gate handcar from the same line. Most active piece of equipment is a Colorado & Southern push car, which is used to haul rails and ties. A wooden baggage truck came from the now-extinct Tonopah & Tidewater.

The Grizzly Flats Railroad has been featured in countless newspaper and magazine write-ups, including in *Life*, and nationwide on TV.

Ward also has a fire truck, together with fire helmets and red shirts for each member of the family to wear while riding it. Once, by chance, they even went to a real fire - and more people stopped to look at them than at the blaze. There'd been a birthday party for one of the Kimball youngsters, and Ward was taking his guests home on the fire truck, which also pulls an antique before-the-turn-of-the-century steam pumper. They heard the modern counterpart coming down the boulevard and turned down a side street to get out of the way. The Los Angeles County fire truck turned down the same street, and before Ward could escape, his vehicle was hemmed in by hundreds of feet of hose.

Personally, Ward is of average height and weight, with hazel eyes and a developing bald spot. He keeps physically fit by doing Yoga nearly every day, including five minutes of head standing. Also, swimming, tennis, and badminton. Sleeps about six hours a night, naps briefly at noon.

Like most of the *Interesting Railfans* in our series, he never smokes, in this case influenced by the bad example of his father having been a chain smoker. Betty doesn't smoke, either. In fact, Ward Kimball never liked to go out with a girl who smokes.

Now and then he lectures on space, art, and movie-making, and has made many TV appearances. The dozen LP albums featuring his "Firehouse 5 Plus 2 Dixie' jazz band are sold all over the world. The Kimballs are animal lovers. Their menagerie boast two Siamese cats, two finches, one lizard, three Mallard ducks, two Coral King snakes, and even a sweetwater Japanese crab.

Ward's pet peeves include phoney politics, insurance salesmen, steam-or-nothing railfans, unchained police dogs, freeway traffic, newspaper society pages, and the dearth of controversial or stimulating TV programs. Politically, he is "slightly left of center."

Says he: "I love long periods of silence: no noise, no talking, no TV, no radio. My favorite relaxation is to stretch out on a hot sandy beach and watch the crowds, seagulls, and girls go by."

His memberships include the Railway & Locomotive Historical Society, four other railfan groups, and four unions in the entertainment field. Ward likes to clown. His sense of humor is sharp, often sardonic.

Last year a 64-page book of his was published, *Art Afterpieces*, that consists of page reproductions of classic paintings by old masters in full color, each picture deftly retouched to give it a saucy or sophisticated slant. For example, Titian's *Allegory*, painted almost 500 years ago, shows a Medieval gentleman looking down over a naked woman's shoulder; Kimball slyly injected a $10 bill into his hand. The retoucher also made Whistler's Mother watch television and gave Mona Lisa a modern hair-do. Such outrages would never be forgiven by art lovers of the old school, but modern devotees find them diverting. *Art Afterpieces* may be seen on pocketbook racks all over the country.

Railfan No. 28 likes to play around with modern art, too, but not the sort that the average person fails to grasp. "I do mechanized paintings," he says, "that are built with moveable parts." One of them, Beauty Machine, is the pliable portrait of a girl which can be made attractive or not by moving her eyes and lips a fraction of an inch.

"Kimball is an uncommon man to begin with," comments the *Independent Star-News* of Pasadena, Calif., "so nothing which rolls out of his workshop surprises his friends and colleagues."

Says Ward, "I'm the kind of guy who likes to cram as much as possible into every 24 hours."

CHAPTER SIX

WALT DISNEY WORLD

THE *VERY FIRST* HIDDEN MICKEY

Hidden throughout all of the Disney theme parks around the world are what are known as "Hidden Mickeys", small secretly placed references to Mickey Mouse. Hidden in the clouds, painted into the bark of a tree, cut into a ventilation grate, or formed as part of the pavement, thousands of these tributes to Mickey can be found in various forms, the most common of which being the "classic 3-circle" Hidden Mickey.

Through the years, I've read many times about *where and when* the very first Hidden Mickey came to be, but I've never read about *how* it came to be. While interviewing Disney Imagineer Terry Peterson about a story element found within Disneyland, he mentioned he had another piece of information that I might be interested in...*the story of how the very first Hidden Mickey came to be*, which happened at Epcot in Walt Disney World...

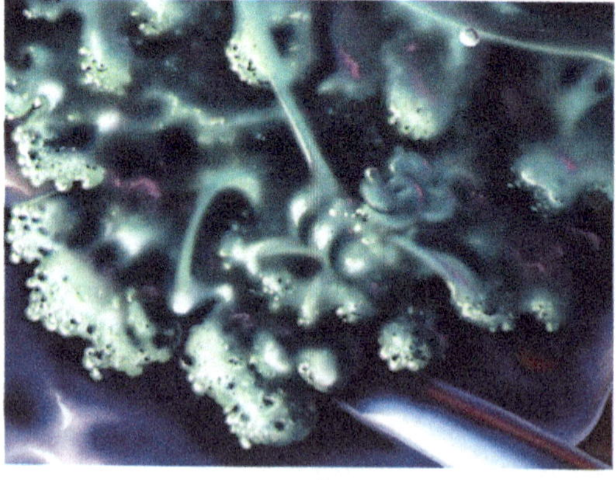

"The nugget I'd most like to share is that I am the one that started the 'Hidden Mickey' gag. It has gotten blown out of proportion, but it all started with my sense of how funny it would be to find (after careful scrutiny) Mickey Mouse in the most incongruous place. I was assigned to paint a 20' high by 100' wide mural of the synapses of the brain for the "Body Wars" ride in the "Wonders of Life" attraction at Epcot. In the upper left section, there was a glob of green broccoli-looking

matter and in that organic abstraction was a two square foot area that looked like Mickey's head. That was the spark that started it all. I turned it into a very realistic head of Mickey, complete with a bit of body and spaghetti-ish limbs, reaching out and blending in with the design. When I was done, as per custom, the one and only John Hench came in to look it over and give final approval. He said "OK, great, nice work.", and I said, "I just wanna show you this first." and explained what I'd done. I said it was only paint and I just thought it would be something only the rider operators would ever see, and I could make it go away in five minutes. He said, "No, leave it. I love it!"

Hidden Mickey photo courtesy of Terry Peterson

ANOTHER ORIGINAL HIDDEN MICKEY

Years ago, there existed a small Hidden Mickey tucked into a large mural within the Maelstrom boat ride of the Norway pavilion. While it was a classic Hidden Mickey known to many, very few know of its backstory, as told to me by its creator, Disney Imagineer Terry Peterson...

"I and three colleagues painted this 20' x 100' mural, which featured all four of us as the giant figures in the piece. While painting the Viking ship, full of men returning from their plundering, I thought it would be funny to replace one of the horned helmets with a Mickey Mouse hat that guests can purchase and wear. I inscribed it with the embroidered name "Leif", and it passed the buyoff and went on to become another fun "inside" joke." *Hidden Mickey photo courtesy of Terry Peterson*

Dispelling a Myth About The Magic Kingdom's Liberty Bell

Found near the Liberty Tree in *Walt Disney World's Magic Kingdom* is a life-sized replica of the historic Liberty Bell, the original of which hangs today in the Liberty Bell Center in Independence National Historical Park in Philadelphia, Pennsylvania.

Around the top of the bell are the words...

PROCLAIM LIBERTY THROUGHOUT ALL THE LAND UNTO ALL THE INHABITANTS THEREOF LEV. XXV. V X – BY ORDER OF THE ASSEMBLY OF THE PROVINCE OF PENSYLVANIA FOR THE STATE HOUSE IN PHILAD.A

Astute guests will notice that the word "Pensylvania" appears to be misspelled on the bell. However, this isn't a mistake, but instead it's another example of Disney's level of attention to historical detail found throughout Liberty Square and Disney theme parks around the world.

So how did this spelling come about originally?

In 1751, the Pennsylvania Assembly sought to obtain a large bell that could be heard all throughout the small but growing town of Philadelphia, as the current bell, purportedly brought to America by William Penn and hung in a tree outside the meeting place of the Pennsylvania colonial assembly, was proving to be too small to be heard all the way to the town's limits when rung. In turn, the Assembly commissioned London's Whitechapel Bell Foundry to cast the new bell, which was to be known as the Pennsylvania State House Bell. Messrs. Isaac Norris, Thomas Leech and Edward Warner all signed the commission for the bell and directed that it should be "...shipped with the following words well shaped in large letters round it viz"...

BY order of the Assembly of the Province of Pensylvania for the State house in the City of Philad.a 1752 - Proclaim Liberty thro' all the Land to all the inhabitants thereof Levit. XXV. 10.

So at the hand of Messers. Norris, Leech and Warner, the spelling of Pensylvania with only two "n"s originated, as this was considered to be acceptable at that time.

Shortly after the bell's arrival in Philadelphia, it was discovered that the bell had suffered a crack, either in transit to America or upon its first ringing. Instead of having the bell shipped back to the Whitechapel Foundry, the Pennsylvania Assembly commissioned two Philadelphia men, John Pass and John Stow, to create an entirely new bell using the metal of the original one. Lacking the proper facilities of the Whitechapel Foundry, the two men broke the original bell into smaller pieces, melted them down and then recast the new bell with a similar design, though with a slightly different inscription, which read:

PROCLAIM LIBERTY THROUGHOUT ALL THE LAND UNTO ALL THE INHABITANTS THEREOF LEV. XXV. V X – BY ORDER OF THE ASSEMBLY OF THE PROVINCE OF PENSYLVANIA FOR THE STATE HOUSE IN PHILAD.A

PASS AND STOW

PHILAD.A

MDCCLIII

Upon the new bell's completion, it was hung in the tower of the State House, later known as Independence Hall. However, the citizens of Philadelphia did not like the tone of the new bell, so they requested Pass and Stow recast the bell once again. The second casting was a success, and it was this second bell that would go on to become known worldwide as the Liberty Bell.

22 Shiny New Liberty Bell Replicas - 1950 - Paccard Fonderie, France

It is interesting to note that many Liberty Bell replicas, including the one in the Magic Kingdom, make the claim that they were cast from the same mold as the original Liberty Bell of either 1751 or 1752. However, this is highly unlikely, as bells manufactured in the mid-1700s were cast using fragile molds made of clay, horse hair, loam and horse manure, and in the case of the Pass and Stow bell, the mold using these elements was formed within a hole dug into the ground. Because the original 1751 bell and the ensuing Pass and Stow bell of 1752 had not achieved historical significance at the time of their casting, it is highly unlikely that much thought would have been given to keeping either of these original fragile molds, let alone arranging to have them preserved for well over 200 years so they may be used in the 20th century. If this were to have occurred, then these same molds would still be preserved today, yet the molds, or even photos of them, do not exist.

Part of the confusion arises from a number of replicas made of the 1752 Pass and Stow bell. In 1950, President Harry Truman created a savings bond campaign to pay for the casting of approximately 56 Liberty Bell replicas by the Paccard Fonderie in Annecy Le Vieux, France. These replicas were created from all new molds, using the Pass and Stow Liberty Bell as a *guide*, and because they were created by the large and well-equipped Paccard Foundry in 1950 instead of two men in a small foundry in 1752, the new bells exhibited a more polished and refined exterior, differing greatly from the somewhat crude and rough exterior of the original Pass and Stow Liberty Bell. Guests will notice that the Magic Kingdom's Liberty Square Liberty Bell, which was cast in 1989, reflects the more refined exterior of its contemporary casting.

Source: My interview with Robert Giannini III - Museum Curator - Independence National Historical Park - Philadelphia, PA

"The Liberty Bell of Independence National Historical Park: A Special History Study - John C. Paige.

Liberty Bell photo courtesy of Dave Drumheller.

1950 Postcard photo of 22 Liberty Bells - Author's collection

A Dreadful Magic Kingdom Murder Mystery

As you enter the interactive queue outside of the Haunted Mansion, you'll come upon a dreadful murder mystery. Perched atop their pedestals are five busts featuring eccentric members of the Dread family, and found in the middle of them all is the bust of Uncle Jacob, the patriarch of the family who, through his exceptional greed, acquired a great deal of money...the kind of money the members of his family would kill for, which is exactly what happened! But the question is... "Who killed who?" Can you solve the mystery using the subtle clues provided? In the copy that follows, I'll walk through the evidence to reveal the killers, while offering up a brand new twist at the end that may or may not be true!

Uncle Jacob

His epitaph reads: "*Greed was the poison he had swallowed. He went first, the others followed. His killer's face he surely knew. Now try to discover who killed who.*"

Holding a large pile of bills and coins, it's clear how wealthy Uncle Jacob was, as well as just what caused his demise. According to the plaque affixed on the pedestal below his bust, he was poisoned by someone he knew, which would likely have been a devious family member *who had access to lethal poison.*

Bertie

His epitaph reads: "*Avid hunter and expert shot. In the end, that's what he got.*"

Here, two important clues stand out; 1) The small icon atop his plaque is that of a bottle featuring a skull and crossbones, certainly filled with poison, and 2) Coiled around his neck, as if a partner in crime, is a large venomous snake, one from which Bertie could extract poisonous venom. All clues point to Bertie as being the one who killed Uncle Jacob. Now all Bertie had to do was poison the remaining family members, and the money would be all his. As fate would have it, however, he never had a chance to, since someone expertly shot him dead. But who???

Aunt Florence

Her epitaph reads: "*Never did a dishonorable deed. Yet found face down in canary seed.*"

With a flintlock pistol adorning her plaque, it's pretty clear that Aunt Florence is the one who shot Bertie. With Bertie dispatched, she then turned her attention to plotting the deaths of the remaining family members, but unfortunately for her, murders of a feather appear to flock together, and soon Aunt Florence was knocked from her perch as next in line to inherit Uncle Jacob's wealth. So, who did the knocking???

The Twins - Wellington & Forsythia

The twins' epitaph reads: "*Departed life while in their beds. With identical bumps on their heads.*"

Adorning Aunt Florence's lapel is a flower held in place by a large stick pin, and adorning the top of that pin is a small bird. This is a clue that she was a fan of birds, an interest exploited by none other than Wellington & Forsythia. Aunt Florence's manner of death was to be found face down in canary seed. The key here is to find the source of the canary seed. Find the seed, and you've found the killer, or in this case "killers", since tucked at the base of the busts of Wellington & Forsythia is a small bag of canary seed. With Bertie and Aunt Florence out of the way, all the twins had to do now was plot the demise of Cousin Maude, and Uncle Jacob's vast wealth would be all theirs!

Cousin Maude

Her epitaph reads: "*Our sleeping beauty, who never awoke. The night her dreams went up in smoke.*"

Now, here's where the story gets interesting, and I'd like to introduce a twist that has not been proposed before...

Look carefully at Cousin Maude's plaque, and you'll see a hammer displayed at the top. This is the murder weapon used to kill the twins, who *died in their beds with identical bumps on their heads.* Their demise would leave Cousin Maude as the sole heir of uncle Jacob's money, except for one thing...she died in her sleep when she caught on fire. How did this happen? If you look closely at the back of Cousin Maude's hair, you'll find three stick matches tucked among her curls. No doubt these rubbed together while she was dreaming of her soon-to-be riches, and her greedy aspirations then went up in smoke.

That's the commonly held and repeated end of the story. However, I don't think the mystery ends here. I find it odd that all of these nefarious family members creatively plotted each other's demise, yet the Disney Imagineers had Cousin Maude passing away simply by accident. I don't think they gave up on the storytelling without tying the loose ends together. Instead, I think she met her fate just as the others had, at the hands of a greedy scheming family member, or two. Here's how...

Look back at the plaque for The Twins. There at the top you'll see a *dead* canary. It turns out that canaries were commonly afflicted with lice, which left untreated, would kill the poor birds. In addition, Cousin Maude was a bit of a firebug, as evidenced by the portrait of her found within the Haunted Mansion with a fire raging behind her. I believe the twins gave Cousin Maude a canary infested with lice, which they knew would infect her scalp and hair. In turn, they also knew that, being obsessed with her own beauty and appearance, she would then employ the old-fashioned (and very unsafe!) remedy of dousing her hair in kerosene before going to bed in an effort to kill the lice. With her habit of keeping a few matches in her curls, the twins knew that once they gave her the lice-infected canary, it was only a matter of time before she treated her hair, the matches rubbed together and ignited...and they had Uncle Jacob's vast wealth all to themselves. Unfortunately, while they lay sleeping, Cousin Maude did them in, perhaps on the same night the twin's flammable scheme played out!

So, with all of the family members meeting a creative demise...whatever happened to Uncle Jacob's riches? Is it all still hidden within the Haunted Mansion???

THE TUMBLEWEED CABINET & CASKET CO.

While hanging onto your hat and glasses when riding the Magic Kingdom's Big Thunder Mountain Railroad attraction, you'll careen past the Explosives Shed with its open cases of Lytum & Hyde dynamite stacked outside. You may notice that placed atop the shed is a casket promoting the *Tumbleweed Cabinet & Casket Co. - Furniture, Upholstery & Embalming.* At first glance, the services offered seem to be simply a whimsical combination of occupations chosen by the Disney Imagineers. However, this is actually an accurate historical depiction of a common practice found throughout the west, including in Walt's hometown, Marceline, Missouri.

Appearing on the brick façade of the historic Zurcher building in Marceline, facing West Richie Avenue, is a large brightly painted advertisement for Coca-Cola, known to all in town as the "Coke Wall". (Page 34) Dating back to 1906, it encourages passersby to drink *Delicious and Refreshing Coca-Cola*...for only 5 cents. Found atop the Coke Wall, in a manner similar to the *Tumbleweed Cabinet & Casket Co.*, is a painted black and white banner promoting *Hutcheson's Furniture & Undertaking*. It was at Hutcheson's, located in the building adjacent to Zurcher's, that Walt's brother, Roy, had secured for the two of them a job cleaning a horse-drawn hearse while the boys were still quite young.

At first glance, it would seem the occupations of furniture making and undertaking would be rather disparate. However, it turns out their combination is quite logical. In the days of the Wild West, small towns didn't have large enough populations to keep undertakers busy on a regular basis, so, given they were skilled in the art of crafting wooden caskets and coffins, undertakers would use these same skills to make and sell furniture to supplement their income.

It's interesting to note that Hutcheson's wasn't the only undertaker in Marceline to engage in this practice, however. In the photo below, you'll find a September 6, 1911 ledger entry for *James McLaughlin FURNITURE AND UNDERTAKING, Marceline, MO.* Here, a mortician in Walt's home town has entered his sale of a dressing table chair, a bed room rocker, a hall rack, another rocker, and a suit parlor, all for $95.85.

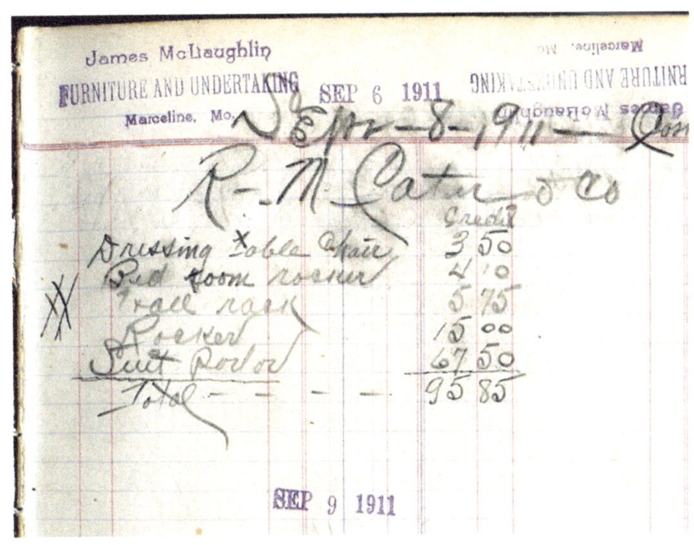
James McLaughlin
FURNITURE AND UNDERTAKING SEP 6 1911
Marceline, Mo. Sept-8-1911

R-M Cater & Co

	Credit
Dressing Table Chair	3 50
Bed Room rocker	4 10
Hall rack	5 75
Rocker	15 00
Suit Parlor	67 50
Total	95 85

SEP 9 1911

Chapter Seven

Disneyland

THE CAPITOL OF DISNEYLAND

Until recently, guests would notice in the foyer of Disneyland's *Great Moments with Mr. Lincoln* attraction a large and magnificently detailed model of our National Capitol Building. Many guests incorrectly assumed this was designed and built by Disney Imagineers for the *Great Moments with Mr. Lincoln* attraction, but it actually has a history that pre-dates Disneyland by more than 20 years. What follows here is the first-ever published account of how this model was created, as well as how Walt came to own it.

Made of Caenstone, this highly detailed model was sculpted by Mr. George H. Lloyd, who was born in March of 1879 in Llanelly, South Wales. As a young man, Mr. Lloyd learned the techniques of stone sculpting and engraving from his father before immigrating to Canada via steamship in 1907, eventually settling in Ottawa. Highly skilled at the art, he practiced his trade on such stately buildings as the Cathedral of St. John the Devine and The Rockefeller Church, both in New York, McGill University in Montreal, and the Canadian Parliament Building in Ottawa, Canada. Mr. Lloyd stated the inspiration for creating his model of the U.S. Capitol Building "*...came to me in 1918 when I saw a picture of the capitol in a Philadelphia paper. I didn't have time to work on the model until the depression when I was out of work.*"

In 1932, only a few years after Mickey Mouse made his debut in Steamboat Willie and 23 years before Disneyland opened, 53 year-old Mr. Lloyd journeyed to Washington D.C. to meet with the Capitol's architect, Mr. David Lynn, where he explained his intent to carve an intricate miniature reproduction of the building out of Caenstone, a fine-grained limestone quarried from the Caen area of Normandy, France. Impressed by Mr. Lloyd's plans, Mr. Lynn graciously supplied him with pictures, drawings, and blueprints, which would not only make the model easier to sculpt, but would ensure its accuracy, as well. With these materials in hand, Mr. Lloyd began the slow and deliberate task of hand-carving over 500 pieces out of stone, a process of intricate craftsmanship which would require many 16 hour days over the course of over three and a half years to finish, resulting in the magnificent structure we see today.

Cathedral of St. John the Devine - New York

In 1940, nearly five years after he had finished, Mr. Lloyd began touring the country while displaying his Capitol model in the department stores of cities large and small, including Chicago, Memphis, Portland, Salt Lake City, San Francisco and Los Angeles, among others. In this era, during the remainder of

Photo courtesy of Jordan Sallis
Mr. Lloyd's great, great, great niece

the Great Depression and before the advent of widespread television, a patriotic and notable achievement such as this would be a form of quality entertainment, and people would journey from miles around to come see it. Over the years, millions of Americans did come to view its stately beauty, and one of those was Walt Disney himself. Being both patriotic and a fan of detailed miniatures, Walt engaged in correspondence with Mr. Lloyd about buying his model with the intention of putting it on display near the entrance of a new "land" he was adding to Disneyland, called "Liberty Street".

On October 18, 1955, Mr. Lloyd was displaying his model in Robinson's Department Store in Southern Los Angeles and wrote to Walt to see if "*...you are still interested in my replica of the National Capital*" (sic). Walt and Mr. Lloyd agreed to terms, and the following Monday, October 24, 1955, Walt had the U.S. Capitol Building model he wanted for "Liberty Street" in the Studio.

Photo courtesy of Jordan Sallis

Mr. Lloyd would later write to his family...

"I displayed my work in Los Angeles...and sold it to a well known motion picture man named Walt Disney and it will be on permanent display at his wonderful exhibition grounds at Los Angeles."

Unfortunately, Liberty Street was never completed, yet the U.S. Capitol Building model was eventually displayed with the *Great Moments with Mr. Lincoln* attraction beginning in 1965, where it was enjoyed by the millions of guests from around the world who visited Disneyland, until its removal in 2025.

Mr. Lloyd passed away in Palo Alto, California in May, 1962 at the age of 82.

An extremely rare June, 1944 brochure distributed by Lowenstein's Department Store in Memphis, Tennessee.
Author's Collection

Mr. Lloyd's words from his World War II era promotional brochure titled, "George H. Lloyd's Hand Carved Caenstone Model of Our National Capitol"...

"I made up my mind to some day carve a model from stone and accordingly went to Washington D.C. where I met Mr. David Lynn, the Capitol architect, who treated me with great kindness. I explained my project and to my great delight, Mr. Lynn made available to me numerous photographs, drawings, and blueprints that made the task much easier and insured accuracy. It has taken me 3 1/2 years to complete my model but I have enjoyed every minute of it, and feel that many thousands of people who have perhaps never visited the Capitol will look with interest and pleasure at this work."

Note: In visiting Disneyland, I wondered about the history of the miniature hand carved stone model of the U.S. Capitol Building on display within the *Great Moments with Mr. Lincoln* attraction, as well as the man who created it. Little to nothing about either was available anywhere, and the plaque affixed to the model at Disneyland offered only a small amount of information. I turned to the web to begin my research and there I found an image of an original World War II era brochure, which was for sale on eBay. Issued by Lowenstein's Department Store in Memphis, Tennessee, it promoted the display of the U.S. Capitol Building model by Mr. Lloyd in their store in June of 1944. That in itself was interesting, but even more so was the first-ever photo I had seen of Mr. Lloyd. The photo showed not only him, but also the U.S. Capitol Building model now found at Disneyland. This was truly a rare and obscure document tied to the history of Disneyland! I placed my bid and then began the wait for the auction to end. Would other people know the significance of this item? Would most people assume it's just an old brochure and overlook it? Does anyone even know who George H. Lloyd is? Thankfully, the auction ended and I was the sole bidder. The price I paid...$5.50.

As I had hoped, upon its receipt the brochure offered up a great deal of never-before-seen information about Mr. Lloyd, as well as additional clues to follow as part of my research, and I am happy to share that with you here.

Lastly, inside the brochure is a hand stamped address for Mr. Lloyd that reads...

GEORGE LLOYD
30 Irving Street
SAN FRANCISCO 22, CALIF.

Note: *I would like to recognize the contribution of Ms. Jordan Sallis, who, along with her grandfather, Brian Hillman, generously shared information and photos which greatly contributed to this story about the Capitol of Disneyland.*

THE DISNEYLAND NEWS

The Disneyland News

OFFICIAL PUBLICATION — DISNEYLAND CALIFORNIA

VOL. 1—No. 1 JULY 1955 10c Per Copy

50,000 ATTEND GALA PARK OPENING.

Celebrities, Officials Join Walt Disney To Dedicate New Era in Entertainment.

California Governor's Message.

Disneyland A 20 Year Dream.

Famed Cartoon Character Creator Long Envisioned Park Where Young And Old Could Find Happiness.

Congress Informed About Magic Kingdom.

'Disneyland News' Off Presses Today.

Year's Subscription Offer Available.

The Disneyland News - Vol. 1 - No. 1
The rare unfolded copy you see here was bought by 11 year old Cathie Moree Rogallo when she visited Disneyland during the park's opening week in 1955.
Author's Collection

Disneyland's Main Street, U.S.A. represents turn-of-the-20th Century America. In this time, before the invention of radio or television, the primary means for obtaining news was the local newspaper, and every town across the country had one, be it The Times, The Tribune, The Gazette, or even the Picayune. Newspapers were big business and a very integral part of any town, large or small.

Walt knew Disneyland would be a very busy place with plenty of news to report. Tales of great danger would come from the deepest reaches of Adventureland, while reports of rocket ships launching for the moon from Tomorrowland would ignite the imagination, and accounts of harrowing escapes in Frontierland would captivate all who heard them. To convey all of this news, Walt wanted a monthly newspaper, something that captured the essence of the 1890s for Main Street, U.S.A., where it would be sold, yet also all the news of today...and that newspaper was *The Disneyland News.*

In June of 1955, Walt hired Marty Sklar, a 21 year-old junior at UCLA and editor of the university's student newspaper, *The Daily Bruin,* and charged him with the task of coming up with an idea for the layout and execution of *The Disneyland News,* and then presenting it to him.

"I went to work at Disneyland in mid-June, 1955 after my junior year at UCLA. Two weeks later, I had to present the concept for The Disneyland News to Walt Disney. Fortunately, he liked it. Then we had to get it written, organized, designed and printed for Opening Day. Much of the written material for the first issue had been developed earlier by the Disneyland Publicity Department. I wrote some new material, organized it, laid out all the pages, and interfaced with the printer. Fortunately, I knew a print shop to use in LA: they printed the UCLA student newspaper. We also found a print shop in Hollywood that had the old wood block type-faces we wanted to use for headlines. And I got support from Jack Jungmeyer, a Disney Studio publicity writer who wrote the wonderful 'Under the Gaslights' column." - Source: My interview with Marty Sklar

Soon, Vol. 1 - No. 1 of *The Disneyland News* was ready, and on Disneyland's opening day, July 17, 1955, it hit the newsstands for all of Disneyland's new guests to read and enjoy for only 10 cents a copy. From the front page of the Vol. 1 - No. 1 first edition...

Here it is, hot off the presses! It's the first edition of the Disneyland News, official publication of Walt Disney's magic kingdom.

All the answers to how Disneyland was created, the artists responsible for the drawing board work, and features on the four "lands" of the Park, along with articles on other Disney enterprises such as the forthcoming Mickey Mouse TV show, are contained in this and following issues of the publication.

In the early days of Disneyland, services for guests, including restaurants, refreshments, camera products, banking, stroller and wheelchair rentals, etc., were provided by "outside" companies, or lessees. The publishing of *The Disneyland News* was handled by Walt's newly formed Magic Kingdom, Inc., while its distribution was handled by two brothers, Joe and Ray Amendt, who ran Castle News at the park as a lessee. Their shop was located where The Mad Hatter shop is now, at the corner of the Opera House/Lincoln Theater building. Guests could buy *The Disneyland News* there, from newsstands on Main Street, U.S.A. or from newsboys outside the entrance gates to the park.

The front page of Vol. 1 - No. 1 featured a photo of Walt and Mickey Mouse aboard the E.P. Ripley under a headline that read *"50,000 Attend Gala Park Opening."* Beneath, guests could read such stories as *Congress Informed About Magic Kingdom, Disneyland A 20 Year Dream*, and *Celebrities, Officials Join Walt Disney To Dedicate New Era In Entertainment.*

Inside its 24 pages were numerous articles about Disneyland's different attractions, how the park was built, the story book adventures of Fantasyland, a new Mickey Mouse newsreel, the upcoming Disneyland

Hotel, and much more, as well as ads for the different businesses found within the park, including Swift Market House, the Wonderland Music Store, Ruggles China and Gift House, the Red Wagon Inn, Yale Lock Shop, The Emporium and many others.

Of course, *The Disneyland News* was part of the story that is Disneyland, and as such, it not only informed guests, but also entertained them, and what could be more entertaining than to see your own name in the headline on the front page of *The Disneyland News*?! For 25 cents, guests could step into the Castle News shop in the Town Square and ask to have their name added to one of a handful of custom headlines, including "...Blasts Off For Moon", "...Visits Disneyland", "...Meets Davy Crockett!", and more.

Of all the stories within *The Disneyland News*, however, the best news of all was that guests across the country could now have their own annual subscription, as well as an informative Disneyland souvenir, delivered right to their front door at home for only $1.20!

Note: Marty Sklar re-enrolled at UCLA in September of 1955 to complete his senior year. He then returned to work for Walt after he graduated and in time became the head of Walt Disney Imagineering, as well as the President and then Vice Chairman and Principal Creative Executive for The Walt Disney Company.

Rare Disneyland Newspaperboy Tour Patch
Author's Collection

DISNEYLAND – A FABULOUS NEW WORLD

Disneyland . . .

. . . A Fabulous New World Is Being Created By Our Friend and Brother Live Steamer . . .

By Dick Bagley

WALT DISNEY'S OLD TIME RAILROAD

YOU CAN BUILD THIS BEAUTIFUL OLDTIME LOCOMOTIVE

The Miniature Locomotive Company

The Miniature Locomotive Magazine - July, 1954 Edition
Author's Collection

Dick Bagley played an important role in not only helping to build Walt's Lilly Belle under the supervision of Roger Broggie, but also Disneyland's C.K. Holliday and E.P. Ripley steam locomotives, as well as the engines of the Mark Twain Riverboat. The following is from an article he wrote about Walt's new theme park for his fellow live steam enthusiasts in his *The Miniature Locomotive* magazine of July, 1954...

Disneyland...A Fabulous New World is Being Created By Our Friend and Brother Live Steamer...Walt Disney

The spirit of adventure has always moved people to explore new lands. In our present age the dream is of rocket ships and new planets, but the object of the quest is the same as ever: a land of peace, pleasure and happiness for all.

Such a place will be Disneyland - The $9,000,000 wonderland which is being created by Walt Disney in Orange County. The charms of this fabulous attraction, unlike anything anywhere else in the world, will be clearly understood and treasured in the hearts of children of all ages. The visitor to Disneyland will leave behind the cares and confusions of the world of today and enter a world of yesterday, tomorrow and fantasy.

I am honored to play even a small part in the creation of this massive project, and flattered that I have been asked by some of our readers to make first hand reports from time to time on interesting phases of the development of this unique center.

To start, let me attempt to tell you about Disneyland, although it is impossible to summarize in a few words. It has been defined as "a combination of world fair, playground, community center, museum of living facts and showplace of beauty and magic." It will be divided into four sections: Fantasyland, Frontierland, World of Tomorrow and True-Life Adventureland. Each will have exhibits, displays, rides, amusements and stores that carry out the theme of the particular area. In short, it will be filled with the magic and beauty that only the genius of Walt Disney could create.

Disneyland will be located on 160 acres of ground near the city of Anaheim, California. Approximately 60 acres will be used for the wonderland and the remainder of the space will be parking area for 10,000 automobiles. The opening is scheduled to take place in midsummer 1955. Meanwhile, heads and hands at the studio will be busy shaping the various wonders.

I have been lucky enough to see quite a few of them. There will be stage coaches, scaled-down replicas of those used in the Old West, accurate in every detail and large enough to carry passengers. There will be the giant squid, the sea monster that provides plenty of excitement in Walt Disney's newest movie, "20,000 Leagues Under the Sea." There will be a breath-taking monorail ride. Busy studio people, like Walt, will be able to commute from Burbank to Anaheim by helicopter. And there will be a train. Two trains.

That happens to be my department. Here, as everywhere else, Walt is the guiding light. The efforts of my crew and myself are to give him the railroad he visions.

There will be 6,010 feet of track on an eight-foot high embankment encircling the entire Disneyland. Visitors aboard the trains - one passenger, one freight - will be able to see all the features of the wonderland as they make the grand circular sightseeing tour.

One locomotive will be the same as Walt's 1½ inch scale "Lilly Belle," with which you are already familiar, and the other will be a modern version of the eight-wheeler. Passenger equipment will be the open vestibule type coaches used back in the 1890's and early 1900's. If that sounds too "modern" and comfortable, you can ride on the freight train, where you'll really rough it. You'll be herded through a cattle chute and probably share the space with a sheep or a goat in a cattle car - or you might be lucky enough to grab a perch in the caboose.

Scale for our railroad is 7½ inch to the foot. Track gauge is 36 inches, which gives us the distinction of being the first people ever to build a scaled-down railroad on a full scale. Or let me say it this way: We are following the design of standard gauge equipment and our trains will be much smaller than those commonly seen on a three foot track. Our trains will be cute, too - or else that helicopter may make a special trip to Siberia.

A Fair *Inspiration* for Disneyland

"Disneyland really began when my two daughters were very young. Saturday was always Daddy's Day, and I would take them to the merry-go-round and sit on a bench eating peanuts while they rode. And sitting there, alone, I felt there should be something built, some kind of family park where parents and children could have fun together."

- Walt Disney

Disneyland is not the result of a single dramatic moment of revelation, but instead it reflects countless instances of inspiration, ingenuity, and impressions experienced by Walt throughout his life, from when he was a young boy in Marceline and Kansas City, to his later years when he would travel around the world.

As a young boy in the early 1900s, Walt lived on the family farm in Marceline, Missouri, where he developed an understanding of the personality of animals, the joy of drawing, and a sense of the small town that would ultimately inspire the look and feel of Disneyland's Main Street, U.S.A.

By 1909, Walt and his family had moved to Kansas City, and it was here that he was introduced to the world of amusement parks offering a broad assortment of entertaining attractions, though due to his job delivering twice-daily newspapers, any visits he made to the parks around town were likely infrequent. However, with the stiff competition for patrons, he no doubt saw the large ads the different amusement parks would run on a regular basis in the Kansas City Star, Kansas City Journal, the Times, and elsewhere, each claiming to have the biggest, tallest, or best amusements in all of Kansas City. Swimming was a popular pastime for land-locked Kansas Citians, and knowing few of their guests would ever see the Pacific or Atlantic oceans, the parks tempted visitors with the rare experience of swimming at ocean shore-like beaches accompanied by an abundance of entertaining amusements. Popular Winnwood Beach promised bathers a day at "The Atlantic City of the West", where patrons could enjoy a 1,200' long boardwalk, two towering waterslides, a high diving platform, two exciting roller coasters, a zoo, a dance floor, and more, all surrounding a large 35-acre spring-fed lake perfect for swimming and boating.

Accessible by an interurban rail line, as well as a horse and buggy ride, Fairmount Park claimed to be the largest and best place to swim in Kansas City, with a spring-fed 8-acre lake and spacious bathing beach surrounded by a beautiful garden setting, picnic grounds, and shady groves. In addition, it offered "Real Fireworks" on different occasions, as well as the Giant Dipper, "The Largest Roller Coaster in the World!"

Perhaps nothing made as much of an impression on Walt, however, as bustling Electric Park, Kansas City's own "Coney Island". Located a short 15 block trolley ride south from his 31st Street neighborhood, he and his younger sister, Ruth, would set out for a day of fun and adventure here, experiencing a grand park unlike any other, all in a meticulously landscaped and well-maintained setting similar to what guests find in Disneyland today.

Electric Park Scene - 1900
Missouri Valley Special Collections – Kansas City Public Library

Initially built in 1899 as a promotional tool by Ferdinand, Joseph, and Michael Heim for their Heim Brewing Company, the park was later rebuilt as a larger 27-acre amusement park, situated closer to the growing areas of Kansas City. At the time of its construction, managed electricity was a new "invention", and the average attendee lived in a world still lit by the soft glow of gas lanterns and gas street lamps. As a result, Kansas City at night was quite dark in most areas, so to stroll the

Night Scene · Electric Park · Kansas City, Missouri

grounds of an exciting amusement park lit by 100,000 bright electric bulbs adorning its buildings and many structures was a thrilling new experience for all who visited, one which made park goers feel as if they were walking amidst and experiencing the future!

But Electric Park wasn't reserved for only nighttime spectaculars. It was filled with exciting thrills and adventures during the daytime, as well. As Walt and Ruth explored its many wonders, Walt no doubt marveled at the elaborate merry-go-round, a majestic electric fountain, penny arcades, shooting galleries, a towering electric swing and spinning Ferris Wheel, vaudeville shows, a wooden roller coaster, a music pavilion, a lively dance hall, a German Village, soda fountains and ice cream shops, a "scenic railway" which encircled the park, and more, all capped by "Real Fireworks" every night. Today, from the merry-go-round and soda fountains to the steam trains and nightly fireworks, you can find many of these same attractions at Walt's theme parks around the world.

STAR, SATURDAY, OCTOBER 2, 1909.

AMUSEMENTS. AMUSEMENTS. AMUSEMENTS.

Electric Park Kansas City's Coney Island

DAY AND NIGHT **BEGINS TONIGHT** DAY AND NIGHT

Agriculture! Horticulture! Floriculture! Dairy Farm! Tobacco! Band Concert!

Grand Fair and Exposition

Dog Show! Poultry Show! Band Contest! Bread Contest! Baby Show! Art and Cooking!

Positively the Greatest Old Style Fair Ever given in the Southwest, Including All of Electric Park's Famous Diversions.

Also The Tickler, Scenic Railway, The Shoots, Babbling Brook, The Alligator Farm

Also Grand Display of the Electric Fountain, every night at 9. Alligator Joe's Wedding tomorrow Night

Electric Park ad in the Kansas City Star - October 2, 1909

Note that with its intricate architectural details and thousands of brightly lit bulbs glowing in the night, a stroll today near Disneyland's large Jolly Holiday Bakery Café must be very reminiscent of Walt and Ruth's turn-of-the-century experience at Kansas City's Electric Park.

A Fair *Motivation* for Disneyland

Travels to the great cities and places of Europe, including Paris, Nice, Copenhagen, and Zermatt with its Matterhorn, imbued Walt with even more ideas for Disneyland, as he strolled open boulevards, visited castles, studied the manicured landscaping and parterres, and even took notes about the features he admired at Tivoli Gardens, one of the finest amusement parks of its era.

But it was perhaps the 1948 Chicago Railroad Fair that provided not only additional ideas and inspiration for Walt's long-simmering idea of a theme park, but also the motivation to begin this project, which was now capturing more and more of his attention.

PART THREE
RAILROAD FAIR

Chicago Daily Tribune

CHICAGO'S RAILROAD FAIR OPENS TODAY

BIG PAGEANT WILL DEPICT RAIL HISTORY

Old, New Trains in Major Roles

TRANSPORTATION ANCIENTS MEET STREAMLINED MODERNS ON LAKE FRONT

CARRIERS PUT ON 10 MILLION DOLLAR SHOW

Exhibits Cover 50 Acre Area

Visitor Has Wide Choice for Eating

SYNTHETIC GEYSER TO LET OFF STEAM LIKE OLD FAITHFUL

Ideal Railroad Envisaged by Presidents of 3 Roads

NIGHTLY DISPLAYS OF FIREWORKS WILL BE STAGED AT FAIR

Strip Diesel Engine to Bare Secrets

1948 Chicago Daily Tribune – Opening Day – Chicago Railroad Fair
Author's Collection

Located on a one-mile stretch of shoreline along Lake Michigan and occupying more than 50 acres, the 1948 Chicago Railroad Fair was an elaborate $10 million dollar exhibition celebrating 100 years of railroading history in Chicago and throughout the West. Running from mid-July through Labor Day, the fair attracted over 2 million visitors who took in countless exhibits, shows, and demonstrations sponsored by 38 different railroads, including "Wheels A'Rolling", "...one of the most spectacular outdoor stage productions ever presented in this country." Here, during numerous shows that occurred every day over the course of the fair, 150 actors and actresses, along with 56 oxen and horses, 20 early automobiles, and a collection of colorful stage elements, would re-enact the important moments in the previous 100 years of railroading history, all with a great deal of pageantry.

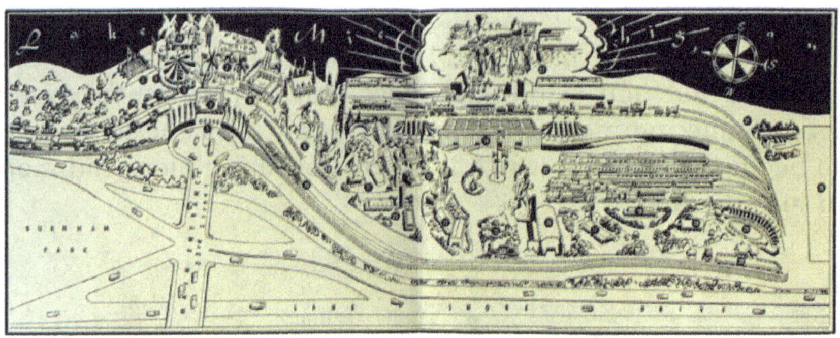

1948 Chicago Railroad Fair Map - From the Official Guide Book
Author's Collection

Back in Los Angeles, Walt was under more and more stress as he dealt with all of the demands of a successful growing studio. His personal nurse, Hazel George, suggested he get away for a while to alleviate some of his stress and to enjoy some much needed relaxation. He knew just the thing...the Chicago Railroad Fair. His wife, Lillian, and his daughters, Sharon and Diane, were sure to have no interest in such an event, so he approached Disney animator Ward Kimball, whom he knew shared his love of trains, and invited him to join him for a trip back east to Chicago to spend a few days immersed in the world of railroading history.

Taking the Super Chief from Pasadena to Chicago, the two were treated as V.I.P.s upon their arrival, and as such they were escorted from exhibit to exhibit as they took in every facet of the entire event. Along the way they ventured behind the scenes, ran prized locomotives, experienced the many exhibits, and asked questions of experts from around the country who shared with them every aspect about the world of railroading.

Inspirations for Disneyland began the moment Walt arrived. Near the main entrance, he saw the *Deadwood Central,* a narrow gauge railway traversing the one-mile length of the fair. Running an old-fashioned steam locomotive with a design like that of the Central Pacific No. 173, the *Deadwood Central* plied the tracks with old-time equipment reflecting railroading as it was in the late 1800s...*including a chattering telegraph instrument at the Central City station,* which is something guests will find today on the Disneyland Railroad.

Nearby was an exhibit presented by the Illinois Central Railroad in which visitors were transported to New Orleans, where they could experience a street scene and patio lifted out of the city's French Quarter. Walt no doubt walked down the quaint narrow streets and through the hidden courtyards, strolled through the tiny shops, noticed the balconies with their ornamental grillwork, and made note of the winding stairway, vine covered walls, and other reflections of the old south, all touches which ended up in Disneyland's New Orleans Square when Walt opened this new land in July of 1966.

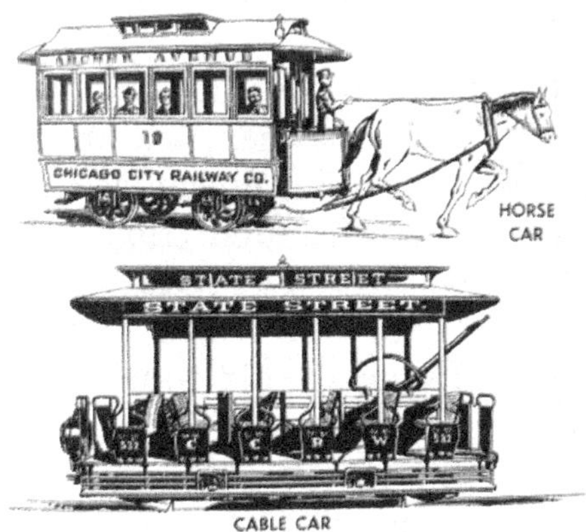

1948 Chicago Railroad Fair Image - From the Official Guide Book

Leaving the New Orleans French Quarter, Walt surely took note of the horse drawn trolleys, fire engines, and other nostalgic vehicles that not only contributed to the festive atmosphere of the fair, but also added a touch of old-fashioned America. Such nostalgic story elements would have resonated with his sense of patriotism and affection for the mid-west, both of which are reflected today on Main Street, U.S.A.

Ad on the back of the 1948 Chicago Daily Tribune
Opening Day - Chicago Railroad Fair
Author's Collection

Near the 5,000 seat grandstand was the "Santa Fe Indian Village." Here, 125 tribesmen, women, and children representing six different tribes presented the culture of Native Americans on the western frontier. Housed in colorful adobe pueblos and other dwellings in a replica of an "Indian Village", including a trading post and curio shop, they performed legendary dances and sang age-old songs during performances given throughout every day of the fair.

In addition to the different exhibits, displays and attractions, Walt may have taken note of the layout of the fair itself. Arranged in a near linear format due to space constraints, the design required visitors to walk back and forth throughout the fairgrounds during their visit in order to catch all of the many different presentations, demonstrations, and shows that occurred at variously scheduled times. This is a format that varies considerably from the efficient hub and spoke layout that Walt chose to use at his Disneyland park.

Greatly enthused by his visit to the fair, Walt wasted no time in moving ahead with his idea for a theme park, for on August 31, 1948, the very next day after he returned to Los Angeles, he wrote a memo to theme park designer and animation art director Dick Kelsey in which he outlined his vision for what would ultimately become Disneyland seven years later. Here are some excerpts from that memo, some of which reflect the same kind of story elements Walt experienced at the Chicago Railroad Fair...

The Main Village, which includes the Railroad Station, is built around a village green or informal park. In the park will be benches, a band stand, drinking fountain, trees and shrubs. It will be a place for people to sit and rest; mothers and grandmothers can watch over small children at play. I want it to be very relaxing, cool and inviting.

The Horse Car. The car would start at the Main Entrance and pick up those who did not want to walk. The car would take them down the street to the Railroad Station. The car would stop here for those who wanted to get off at the village or they could continue on to the Western village, then loop around and come back by way of the Carnival section; then on to the Main Village for a stop and continue until it was back at the Main Entrance.

We will have a Livery Stable where buck-boards are for hire. These will carry adults and children and will be pulled by a team of ponies which would drive them all around the village. Surreys and buck-boards will be available to go through the Western Village and the old farm. In other words, they can use any road. They will be rented by the half-hour, including the driver.

The Western Village. A general store with a soda fountain and lunch counter. We could sell most of the articles we have in the drug store in the village but we would also sell Western toys, Western outfits, toy guns, etc.

The Stage Coach. The coach would leave from the Western Village, pass through the farm, go through the Indian village and pass the old mill. This would be by a special road.

The Donkey Pack Train. The donkeys would be all hooked together and handled by one man. This would take ten kids.

For the next eight years, the idea of Disneyland would continue to be on Walt's mind, occupying more and more of his attention with each passing day.

Disneyland Progresses

Early Main Street, U.S.A. Elevation Drawing
As displayed at the Walt Disney Family Museum

Dick Bagley followed up his July, 1954 article with another in the September - October issue of *The Miniature Locomotive Magazine*. In this piece, he gave an update on Disneyland's progress, with the park now less than one year away from its opening date.

Disneyland Progresses

By Dick Bagley

Dreams are now moving swiftly into reality. In many instances they have passed the blueprint stage. During the last month I have seen tiny gasoline automobiles whizzing around the studio lot being tested. Buggies of yesteryear, including stage coaches and surreys - with the fringe on top - are making an appearance.

In a movie studio you become accustomed to seeing strange sights. To find yourself in a setting of 100 years ago is not at all unusual. But to suddenly be confronted with a little red fire engine pulled by small horses as you walk down the street is another matter. For an instant you might think that besides going back 50 years things had also been shrunk.

There is activity everywhere. Walt Disney's workshops are busy. Somehow, I am reminded of the well known stories of the mythical Jolly Old Elf and his workshop in the far north where it is said that he is so busy all year preparing for the happiest of all days, Christmas. Not that I would compare Walt to Santa Claus, that is, except for his kind intentions. And in this respect, I wonder if anyone else has ever come so close to actually giving the people of this world the things for which Santa takes credit.

The Disneyland Railroad is fast taking shape. Two steam locomotives are under construction. Main frames were flame cut from one huge piece of steel. They are two and one-half inches thick and almost 18 feet long. Each weighs 640 pounds. If you have ever machined a set of frames for a small loco, then you would have enjoyed watching the apparent ease with which these frames were handled for finish work in the milling machine.

Many other parts for the locos have also been flame cut from sheet steel. For the benefit of those who may not be familiar with the process I will give a brief explanation. The flame is supplied by an oxy-acetylene cutting torch attached to a traveling crane. Thus the torch can be made to follow an intricate pattern and the whole works is propelled by electric power. Patterns to guide the torch may be made in several different ways. Ours were cut from paper and a photo electric-cell device followed around the edge of the cutout, thus directing the cutting torch. Steel cut in this way is smooth enough as to not require machining except for working surfaces.

Our pattern shop has already turned out a good truckload of the nicest patterns and core boxes that I have ever had the pleasure to see. Nearly all of the patterns required to build the locos have been completed. Most of the castings are also made.

Cylinders and saddles will be finish machined before this reaches print. They are cast in semi-steel. The design consists of three pieces, the two cylinders being separate from the saddle as was on the original full size loco No. 173. Cylinder Bore is ten inches.

Drive wheels are three-foot diameter and weigh 750 pounds each. They are fitted with standard locomotive hard steel tires. The wheel centers are cast in steel from our own pattern. Drive axles are chrome molly ground stock four inches in diameter. Side rods and main rods are also chrome molly. This material was chosen for these hard-working parts because of its great strength and ductile quality.

Engine trucks are made from bar stock in authentic copy of those used at the turn of the century but have been welded together, rather than bolted, to give added strength and safety.

The boilers are being built in a boiler shop according to A.S.M.E. code. They are welded construction. The owners of this shop and also their men have become so interested in our job that we are receiving all sorts of special attention. Everywhere I go the same is true. People in the various shops meet me with pleasure and each visit finds them more interested in locomotives than before. Most of them have never had anything to do with a railroad, but they are learning fast. There must be something contagious about this hobby of ours?

A great deal more has already been done. I would like to tell you about the cute little passenger cars that Walt is planning and lots of other things, but space is running out.

Orchestrating The Story That Is Disneyland

To Walt, so much of the story that is Disneyland was found in the details. Circling his park are his magnificent steam trains, which purposely clank and clatter as they ply the tracks, in the very same manner as the large steam trains he rode as a boy in Kansas. In Adventureland, the animals of the Jungle Cruise aren't static, but instead portray actual live animals with their realistic life-like movements, and on Main Street, U.S.A., the music that fills the air is that of turn-of-the-century rag time played by the coin-operated player pianos, nickelodeons, and orchestrions of that era.

Disneyland is home to two orchestrions, both priceless mint-condition original working models...

The Nelson-Wiggen Orchestrion

Formerly located in the Disneyland Railroad Main Street Station, and now found in Frontierland's Silver Spurs Supplies, is the nearly 100 year-old 1927 Nelson-Wiggen 6 Orchestra Orchestrion. Featuring a piano, xylophone, snare drum, bass drum, banjo, cymbal and many other instruments, this original element of the Disneyland story provides guests with a taste of genuine musical entertainment from the days of when Mickey Mouse was being introduced to the world as Steamboat Willie. Drop in a quarter, and you'll hear a jaunty ragtime tune that differs from the more melodic orchestral tune of the large Welte Style 4 orchestrion found in the Penny Arcade of Main Street, U.S.A.

But how did this rare musical instrument come to find its way to Disneyland? In 1953, when Walt was busy formulating his plans and designs for building his new theme park, he made a visit to Mrs. Ruby Raney, widow of Mr. Albert Clifford Raney, to look at his extensive collection of mechanical music machines, which was one of the largest in the country. With Mr. Raney's passing, she was looking to sell most of his machines, and Walt realized they may be perfect for his vision of Main Street, U.S.A. Upon seeing the collection, Walt was so impressed that he bought 30 different machines, including the rare Nelson-Wiggen orchestrion pictured here.

It's interesting to note that visitors to the Magic Kingdom in Orlando, Florida will also find a similar orchestrion, this one being built by the Seeburg Piano Company, also in 1927. In 1922, two employees of the Seeburg Piano Company struck out on their own to begin making their own orchestrions, unaware their work would one day be seen by millions of people every year in a theme park in California. And their names?...Oscar Nelson and Peder Wiggen.

The Welte Style 4 Orchestrion

Standing in the back of Main Street, U.S.A.'s Penny Arcade is a stunning Welte Style 4 orchestrion, which has been playing music at Disneyland since opening day in 1955. Manufactured in 1907 by M. Welte & Söhne in Freiburg, Germany, this elaborate antique provided the kind of musical entertainment enjoyed by Walt Disney as a child. Its collection of instruments features 265 pipes, as well as a bass drum, snare drum, timpani, triangle and cymbal, all while playing 75 key Welte roll music. Walt purchased this in 1953, and in 1955 it was installed in the Penny Arcade, where it's been entertaining guests ever since...just as Walt intended.

The following history of the Welte orchestrion is courtesy of the Mechanical Music Press. (www.MechanicalMusicPress.com)

From the beginning, Welte orchestrions were the premier automatic musical instrument of choice for royalty and the very wealthy, a trend that began circa 1849, when Michael Welte exhibited his immense automatic pipe organ, receiving generous critical acclaim and numerous awards for the device. At the time, his invention was an astounding advancement in technology, and reportedly the fame of the huge automatic musical instrument drew crowds from near and far. The public nicknamed the instrument "orchestrion", because it successfully imitated a many-voice orchestra. Since that time the term orchestrion has become synonymous with virtually any automatic musical instrument attempting to imitate a small to large orchestral ensemble. Thus it is that Michael Welte's early pioneering accomplishments in building spectacular, mammoth self-playing orchestras paved the way for his company's rapid climb to fame and fortune, with his handsome orchestrions being renowned on a worldwide basis.

Michael Welte began very modestly, after five years of apprenticeship with the master craftsman Joseph Blessing, by opening a small factory in Vöhrenbach, Germany, the town that was his birthplace in 1807. The little factory began business in 1832, with Michael Welte constructing musical clocks and other small musical cabinets on his own. The Welte firm prospered by word of mouth, quickly becoming well known and respected for not only the architectural beauty of its products, but for the quality of workmanship, too. In 1865, Michael Welte's oldest son, Emil Welte, established a Welte showroom in New York City, where he exhibited a number of large orchestrions, along with flute playing clocks, which the company still manufactured in small numbers. Immediately successful, or so it was stated by Welte advertising literature, the addition of the new American showroom, coupled with other already established markets for Welte products, soon compelled the company, in 1872, to move to nearby Freiburg.

By 1905 the line of products grew to include the soon to be acclaimed Welte Mignon Reproducing Piano, as well as retaining many of the older style products, such as the extensive line of Cottage and Concert Orchestrions. During the next few years, Brass Band Orchestrions, Philharmonic Orchestrions, "Brisgovia" Piano Orchestrions, residential pipe organs, theatre organs, home player pianos, and other related items would be added to the Welte roster. All in all, as most historians and enthusiasts of automatic musical instruments will concur, instruments built by Michael Welte & Söhne were among the most eye-appealing, magnificently ornate, and stunningly beautiful of all the large orchestrions manufactured. Thus, it is no wonder that they were so appreciated by the Royalty, wealthy industrialists, and fine commercial establishments that sought the privilege of owning a fine Welte instrument.

The Welte Style 4 Orchestrion - Before Disneyland

Stop and admire the towering 1907 Welte Style 4 orchestrion in the Penny Arcade, and you'll be impressed by its finely polished woodwork, ornate roll player, and shiny brass and nickel pipes, all in better-than-new condition. Walt acquired this grand machine in 1953 from the collection of Mr. Albert Clifford Raney of Whittier, California, and if you're like me, you've always assumed he bought it in a condition similar to what guests see today when they visit the park. Perhaps all the Imagineers had to do to make it show-ready was a bit of cleaning, polishing, and fine-tuning. It turns out that my assumption was incorrect.

Recently, I picked up an out-of-print 1966 edition of the book, *Put Another Nickel In*, hoping to find a rare bit of information relating to Disneyland and its orchestrions. I was pleasantly surprised to discover that the very last page in the book featured a large photo, taken in 1950, which I had never seen before. There, on page 248, was a photo of the very Welte Style 4 orchestrion found in Disneyland today, while it was still in Mr. Raney's collection. Of note is that the photo reflects the orchestrion in the same condition that Walt found it in, with its lower left front panel missing, two side panels cracked, the front glass panels removed, and the entire machine covered in scratches.

Disneyland's Welte Style 4 Orchestrion while still in the Mr. Albert Clifford Raney Collection - 1950 Photo
Photo courtesy of Put Another Nickel In - By Q. David Bowers

Crystal Arts & The Arribas Brothers

Step into the Crystal Arts shop on Main Street, U.S.A., opposite the Gibson Girl Ice Cream Parlor, and you enter into a world of history reaching directly back to Walt and the early days of Disneyland, as well as nearly 100 years ago to the small town of La Coruña, Spain, for it was here that Tomas Arribas was born in 1930, followed by his younger brother, Alfonso, in 1936. As young men they studied the old-world skills of glassblowing, a craft practiced by their family for generations, which was now being passed down to them both. In time, they developed such skill and mastery of the art that they began to acquire a reputation for their fine work, and in 1963 the two of them were approached by the Spanish Cultural Ministry to represent Spain in a pavilion at the 1964 / 1965 Worlds Fair, to be held in New York.

Comprised of three interconnected buildings, the Spanish Pavilion was hailed as the "Jewel of the New York World's Fair", showcasing Spain's rich cultural heritage. Historical artifacts, oil painting masterpieces, priceless sculptures by world-renowned artists, stunning treasures, innovative technology, and of course glassblowing exhibits drew millions of visitors to one of the most popular pavilions at the fair. Among these visitors was Walt Disney himself, and he was so taken by the impressive glassblowing skills and resulting artwork of Tomas and Alfonso, that it was decided that the Arribas brothers would open a glassblowing shop at Disneyland.

The 1964 / 1965 New York World's Fair ran through October of 1965, and in June of 1967, the Arribas brothers opened their first glassblowing studio in a small shop inside Sleeping Beauty Castle. Though tucked out of the way, guests were just as impressed with the glasswork as Walt was, and in time the shop was moved to Main Street, U.S.A., where it has been a classic Disneyland attraction ever since. Today, guests can purchase Disney characters, crystal artwork, intricate pieces of jewelry, impressive large sculptures, shimmering tiaras, and many other hand-crafted souvenirs at 19 different Arribas Brothers shops found at Disney parks and properties around the world.

The Gibson Girl Ice Cream Parlor

Throughout Disneyland you'll find tributes to individuals who greatly influenced Walt Disney's life...the colorful antique mutoscopes acknowledge animator Winsor McCay, a window on Main Street, U.S.A. recognizes Walt's father, Elias Disney, and with every frozen scoop of one of Walt's favorite treats, The Gibson Girl Ice Cream Parlor pays tribute to Charles Gibson.

Charles Dana Gibson was a skilled American illustrator best known for creating the "Gibson Girl", his personification of a woman who embodied feminine beauty and confidence during the late 19th and early 20th centuries, the period depicted on Main Street, U.S.A. His exceptional skills as an illustrator, especially those that conveyed the expressions of the human face in his prodigious work, were recognized and appreciated by millions around the world, including a young Walt Disney.

In addition, during World War I, Mr. Gibson led the Division of Pictorial Publicity for the Committee on Public Information, a government agency charged with influencing public opinion about the war. In this role, Mr. Gibson was involved with assisting military recruitment, and as such he lent his notable creation, the Gibson Girl, to those efforts, including in a poster which encouraged young men to serve in WWI as ambulance drivers in France. Coincidentally, this was the position Walt held after joining the Red Cross Ambulance Corp at the age of 16. As part of his responsibilities, Walt spent about ten months in France, from 1918 to 1919, driving supplies from warehouses to hospitals and canteens in and around Paris, as well as the surrounding French countryside.

Of note is that only two Disney theme parks in the world include a Gibson Girl Ice Cream Parlor; Disneyland and, of course, Disneyland Paris.

Walt as a Red Cross Ambulance Corp driver in France
Photo courtesy of The Walt Disney Family Museum

Fur the Birds, Tuppence a Bag

Opening in June of 1963, Walt Disney's Enchanted Tiki Room was the first attraction to include Walt's new Audio-Animatronic technology, allowing a cast of over 150 talking, singing and dancing birds to entertain guests in a Polynesian setting.

Photo courtesy of Dave Drumheller

Have you ever wondered how Disneyland's Figure Finishing Department adorned all the Audio-Animatronic birds in their bright plumage such that they could move and still appear as real birds? Thirty year Imagineer Cindy Bothner explains the process in this interview, which is presented here with her kind permission...

"Fur and feathering a Tiki Bird is quite involved. If I remember correctly, it takes about 36 hours, maybe less after you get the hang of it. First, you are given a fiberglass and kydex (an alternate to leather) bird body. A pattern is made of muslin for the fur cloth, or bird fur. The pattern has to allow for the movement of the head, but still be snug enough so as not to bunch up and look fake. Very tricky!

You also have to craft a spandex collar that is glued to the neck opening, which keeps the bird fur from folding into the neck area when the bird moves. You then cut out the fur cloth according to the pattern. Before gluing it on, you paint the cloth the desired colors, which are air-brushed on with permanent ink. The face and feet are then painted with water-

based acrylics. After the painting, you glue on the fur cloth and then feather the wings and tail. This is done in a specific pattern using pre-selected feathers that are trimmed just right.

We also had to decorate the cages for the Tiki Room. We were given a cage fabricated from metal tubing. We applied Bondo to the tubing (Bondo could easily be carved to look like wood), and then painted and decorated the cages.

We had a wonderful teacher for the whole Tiki project in Leota Thomas. Leota and Harriet Burns were the Imagineers who furred and feathered the original Tiki Birds for Disneyland, and then later for Walt Disney World.

Leota was originally from the Walt Disney Studios, where she had worked in the Ink & Paint Department. She came over to WED when Disney first started the company. Without this wonderful lady teaching us the intricacies of the Tiki Birds, it would have been very time-consuming to figure out the exact method. She also taught us the use of 'Animal Vinyl Paint', which was used on the flexible bodies of the Animatronic figures, animal and human, as well as the Elephants, Hippos and others in the Jungle Cruise. The paint was actually a liquid form of the skin itself."

FIGARO MAKES AN "EXIT"

In the entry way of Disneyland's Red Rose Taverne in Fantasyland is a whimsical historical story. Placed above two entry way doors is an "Exit" sign. The sign itself is nothing out of the ordinary, but it's placement is, as it is immediately obvious that it is a bit off center from where a sign such as this is usually located, that being in the *middle* above the two doors. In a bit of whimsy, Disney Imagineers have painted Sultan, a character from Disney's animated hit Beauty and the Beast, pulling on a rope attached to the sign in an effort to pull it back into place. However, Sultan has not always been the character depicted here. The Red Rose Taverne used to be the Village Haus restaurant, and the character originally depicted as tugging on the sign was Figaro, Geppetto's cat. The following is the first-ever *complete* story of how Figaro came to be painted here more than 40 years ago, as shared with me by Disney Imagineer Terry Peterson...

The story of the Figaro gag is this: It was 1983, and after painting tons of art that would adorn the walls of the Fantasyland rides as well as the Village Haus restaurant, I and another colleague started the location work of tying in the murals with the 3D elements. After painting the dwarves' cottage and other elements in the Pinocchio load/unload, I was assigned the touch-up and tie-in of my murals going into the restaurant. I noticed that the exit sign was off center, and I knew it was because there was a structural element on center that would not accommodate the recess necessary for the sign housing. Having established a comfortable relationship with the great art director Tony Baxter, I decided to take a chance and paint Figaro starting to pull the sign to its proper spot and giving a wink to those "in" on the joke. When Tony came in the next day I pulled him aside and said, "Look, I did something on my own and if you hate it, I can make it go away in five minutes - it's only paint." He took one look and after figuring what must have happened he said, "NO! I love it, leave it!" Funny enough, the myth surrounding it lived on without me but when the restaurant was duplicated in Paris, (where I contributed much work, but not this) an artist rendered Figaro leaning on the properly placed exit sign, winking and giving the thumbs up. Talk about an inside joke. I loved it!"

Photos courtesy of Terry Peterson

EMILE KURI ACQUIRES DISNEYLAND'S CANNONS

You see them every time you stroll through Town Square...two impressive 3" Hotchkiss Mountain Guns, both manufactured in France sometime during the late 1800s.

Nearly every major story element within Disneyland has an interesting backstory attached to it. However, as I looked into the two cannons found in Disneyland's Town Square, I could find no information at all about their history or how they were acquired, only that Walt wanted to include them in Disneyland as a tribute to the service and sacrifice of America's veterans, in the same manner as the cannon he used to sec as a boy in Marceline's E.P. Ripley Park. However, I persisted in my research, which led me to Disney Legend Emile Kuri's son, John Kuri, who graciously shared with me his father's notes about how he came to acquire these two often overlooked pieces of the Disneyland experience.

Following his Academy Award-winning work creating Victorian masterpieces for the set design used in the 1949 film *The Heiress*, Emile Kuri was hired by Walt Disney in 1952 to be the Head of Decorating - Property Department at Walt Disney

Studios, where he went on to win a second Academy Award for his work in Disney's 1954 classic *20,000 Leagues Under the Sea*, as well as an Emmy in 1963 for his work in *Walt Disney's Wonderful World of Color*.

As the production for *20,000 Leagues Under the Sea* began to wind down, Walt asked Emile to now focus his talents on Walt's new project, Disneyland. It was here that Emile's devotion to detail and storytelling would become evident throughout the park, especially in Town Square and Main Street, U.S.A., where he would practice his craft within the design constraints of forced perspective.

In obtaining the story elements he wanted for Disneyland, Emile scoured the entire country, looking for pieces with not only the correct size, proportion, and design aesthetic, but also, as Disneyland got closer to it's opening day and the budget became strained, the right price, as well.

What follows are Emile's personal notes about how he discovered and acquired the two Town Square cannons...

"Another interesting and hard-to-find item was a pair of field cannons, which I had planned to use in Town Square, one on either corner of the square, facing the entrance to the park. The problem was that the average field cannon is tremendous in size. I had read of a museum in New York that had a large collection of field artillery. On one of my many trips, I went to the museum and found a pair of French field cannons that were just the right size. I spoke with the man in charge and told him where I was from and asked him if I might find two such cannons to purchase and much to my surprise, his answer was 'Right here. We happen to have two more cannons just like these, and since we have no use for them, I would very much like to sell them to you.' I was amazed at my good fortune."

Why Ship Them All The Way From Baltimore?

Walt Disney & Emile Kuri
Photo courtesy of John Kuri

As I researched Walt's life in Kansas City and discovered that his neighborhood was illuminated by gas street lamps, I got to wondering...Why did Emile Kuri ship the gas street lamps he chose for Disneyland's Main Street, U.S.A. all the way from Baltimore, Maryland, when he could've bought and shipped them from the mid-west, perhaps even Kansas City, some 1,500 miles closer, especially when Walt was doing everything he could to save money while constructing Disneyland? With this in mind, I had the good fortune to connect with Emile Kuri's son, John Kuri, who graciously shared with me his father's thoughts on this very issue. At the time of this book's publication, the following *complete* story had been shared by Emile with only his family, as well as placed within the archives of the Margaret Herrick Library, a world-renowned reference and research collection of print, graphic, and research materials dedicated to the Academy of Motion Picture Arts and Sciences. I'd like to thank John for publicly sharing this full account with Disney guests for the first time via this book, *Disney History - Rare & Unknown...*

Perhaps the most difficult segment that I faced in Disneyland were the lighting fixtures. The lamp posts for Main Street and Town Square were a real problem, for the buildings in our turn-of-the-century Main Street were all scaled down in size. The first floor was around seven-eighths scale and the second floor five-eighths scale. Wherever there was a third floor, it was about four-eighths scale. By comparison, the average Main Street lamp post of that period was around twenty to twenty-five feet tall; much too tall for our buildings. We also needed a great number of lighting fixtures for the exterior and interior of the buildings. But in 1955 there were no lighting fixture companies manufacturing reproductions. I visited some factories in New York, Philadelphia and other cities and, in some cases, I found parts of old fixtures in basements. I literally had to beg them to make the chandeliers in the Emporium and the Golden Horseshoe. All the antiques I used became a number one attraction in the world. Every lighting fixture company began making reproductions and the public responded by buying them. We actually created that market.

I purchased lamp posts for Frontierland from San Jose and others from Los Angeles. I drove across the entire country in search of the Main Street lampposts and eventually someone told me that the city of Baltimore was replacing some very old residential gas burning lamps with modern electric ones. I went to Baltimore's City Hall. Carrie Lou most often went with me on these trips. We asked for the location of the old gas-burning posts they were replacing. I could not have been happier when I saw them. They were absolutely perfect, about fifteen feet in height. They had illuminated the streets for 140 years. So back to City Hall where I told them I would like to buy fifty of them and asked their price. I could not believe the clerk's answer. He told me there were planning to sell all the lampposts as scrap iron at the then current price of three cents a pound. He also told me that they did not have the lanterns with the gas burners for the top of the posts, but I could buy them from the city of

Philadelphia. He showed me a picture of the new posts. I just could not understand the city of Baltimore removing those 140 year-old beautiful posts, selling them for scrap iron and then replacing them with ugly modern electric ones. Why not electrify the old ones?

- Emile Kuri

Note: Carrie Lou was Emile Kuri's wife. An extraordinary artist, she was the first female graduate of Hollywood High School to receive a scholarship to the prestigious Chouinard Art Institute. In a world dominated by men at that time, this was a significant and notable ground-breaking achievement on her part, and one which helped to open many doors for the women who followed.

The Story Behind Main Street, U.S.A.'s Hitching Posts

Disneyland's Main Street, U.S.A. captures and holds in guests' hearts and imaginations the years of 1890 through 1910, a romantic old-fashioned period when the grass was greener and life moved at a slower, friendlier pace. However, this was also a period of change, and the Disney Imagineers reflect this in the abundance of story elements surrounding guests as they make their way through Town Square and up Main Street, U.S.A. Electricity was now reaching more and more homes in America, upbeat ragtime music filled the air with a sense of joy and optimism, steam-powered locomotives were opening up the west, and horse and buggies were being replaced with the newfangled gas-powered automobile.

One of the story elements Emile Kuri made sure to include on Main Street, U.S.A. was hitching posts. After all, even though more and more automobiles were filling the streets, he knew plenty of folks would still be riding into town on their horse and buggies to load up on supplies at the Emporium, to pick up some Epsom salts at the Upjohn Pharmacy, or perhaps even to see a silent movie at the Main Street Cinema.

Like so many story elements in Disneyland, the hitching posts of Main Street, U.S.A. have an interesting story behind them, and I'd like to share that story with you here, as it was kindly shared with me by John Kuri, Emile Kuri's son.

In 1947, while working for Paramount Pictures to create the set for the movie *The Heiress*, starring Olivia de Havilland and Montgomery Clift, Emile Kuri traveled to Washington Square in New York City, along with William Wyler, to find a building façade that would be suitable for what he envisioned to serve as the exterior of Dr. Sloper's home, the father of Oliva de Havilland's character, Catherine Sloper. They chose a home that was built in the early 1800s, which was owned by the 80 year-old daughter of the man who had built it. Along the curb in front of this residence were two remarkable hitching posts, both fashioned with the head of a horse. Emile was quite taken by the posts, and he commented to the owner about their stately presence. Seeing how much he appreciated the hitching posts, the owner of the home graciously insisted that he accept one as a gift, and upon Emile's departure, she had the hitching post removed, crated up, and shipped to Hollywood, where Emile installed it in his backyard. Approximately seven years later, when Emile was making decisions for the story elements he wanted on Main Street, U.S.A., he knew exactly what he'd use for the design of the hitching posts he'd include...the very one in his own backyard. Working with the Alhambra Foundry in Los Angeles, he contracted to have 30 replicas made, and these were delivered and installed on Main Street, U.S.A., where they still reside today.

Of note is that Emile Kuri won his first Oscar© for Best Art Direction-Interior Decoration (Black and White) for his outstanding work on *The Heiress*.

Serendipitous Happenstance Times Two

A well-known story about Emile Kuri's good fortune in acquiring the base of the flagpole found in Town Square involves the serendipitous happenstance of Emile arriving upon an accident one day in April of 1955 and seeing that a car had collided with and dislodged a street pole, ruining it in the process. Emile noticed that the street pole's ornate cast iron base had survived the crash, and seeing an opportunity, he asked the crew clearing the debris if he could buy it, which he did through the LA City Public Works Department the next day for 5 cents a pound. In no time, he had it fitted with a flag pole and installed in Town Square, where it has served dutifully in honoring veterans ever since.

The flag pole base isn't the only story element within Town Square with such an interesting story behind it, however. Nearby, only a few paces away, two other items involve a bit of destruction and Emile's serendipitous happenstance in their acquisition. What follows is Emile Kuri's account of how he came to obtain the lamps that light the stairs to the Disneyland Railroad Station, as provided to me by John Kuri...

"Driving down Highland Avenue in front of Hollywood High School, where Carrie Lou, Fred and Betsy had been students, I noticed they were tearing down the old auditorium. I parked my car and climbed the stairs to the entrance, where a man wearing a 'Cleveland Wrecking Company' uniform was standing. Pointing to a pair of seven-foot lamp posts with a cluster of four lights on each, I asked him if they were going to be removed. He said, 'Yeah, everything goes.' I told him I'd like to buy them and he answered, 'They will cost you thirty-five dollars'. I got a receipt and had the truck pick them up the following day. Ever since, they have been illuminating the stairway that leads up to the Santa Fe Railroad Station, just above Town Square."

THE 10 MILLIONTH GUEST OF THE DISNEYLAND RAILROAD

Left to Right - R.G. Rydin, Executive VP of the Santa Fe Railway, Raymond Sleeper, and Walt Disney

Above is an August, 1960 press photo of Walt Disney, R.G. Rydin, and 8 year-old Raymond Sleeper, who, as luck would have it, found himself amid considerable pageantry and fanfare as he became the 10 millionth guest to ride aboard the Santa Fe Disneyland Railroad, a milestone rewarded by Walt when he presented young Raymond with a special one-of-a-kind commemorative boxcar filled with 10,000 pennies. As I recently read about this story, I wondered...whatever happened to Raymond, the boxcar, and all of those pennies? My initial research uncovered very little about him or his big day at Disneyland, so I set out to find Raymond...over 60 years later...to answer these questions. It took some searching, but I found him, and what follows is his story, told for the very first time anywhere...

In mid-summer of 1960, Mr. & Mrs. Sleeper were in the process of moving their young family from Hawaii to Maryland, as Mr. Sleeper, who was a Colonel in the U.S. Air Force, was being transferred to Andrews Air Force Base. Reaching California, the plan was to drive across country in their new baby blue Rambler station wagon, but first a trip to Disneyland was in order. On the morning of August 3rd, the Rambler pulled into the busy Disneyland parking lot, and inside, 8 year-old Raymond, his sister, and his four brothers grew antsy with excitement and anticipation as Disneyland's Main Street Station came into view. This was their very first trip to the park. Little did they know, they were about to experience a special moment of Disney magic, one which they would all remember for the rest of their lives.

Piling from the car, Raymond and his siblings all gazed upon the majestic train station gleaming in the California sunshine high above the entrance gates. Guests gathered in line at the turnstiles to get into the park, and somewhere in the distance a train whistle announced the impending arrival of the Ernest S. Marsh locomotive, finishing yet another journey from such distant places as Adventureland, Frontierland, Tomorrowland, and beyond. Raymond remembers what happened next...

"I recall my father saying, 'We should ride the railroad around the park first, to get an idea of what we can see and what we want to do for the day.'

Once inside, my two younger brothers and I raced for the Santa Fe & Disneyland Railroad Station. I was 8 and arrived first at the turnstile for the next train, followed by my younger brother, Harry, who was 6, and my youngest brother, Grant, who was 5. When the rest of the group arrived, I let Grant get in front of me so that he could be first in line. Seeing this, Harry began grumbling about his being younger than me, so I let him in front of me, too. It was then that I noticed that the ticket takers and others seemed to be paying close attention to us as we waited in line, talking to each other as they kept an eye us. When we were let through the turnstile, some cast members pulled us all aside and began excitedly speaking to my parents, letting them know that something special had just happened...I was the 10 millionth guest on the Santa Fe & Disneyland Railroad, and I was about to be awarded a magical prize, a unique box car filled with 10,000 pennies, along with a Revell HO model railroad set!

Raymond Sleeper receives a special HO scale model train and layout from Walt Disney
Photo: Don Erb - Santa Fe Railway

Shortly after they spoke with my parents, they approached me and told me that I was a special guest for the day, one who had just won 10,000 pennies, which was a lot of money for an 8 year-old boy. In addition, I was named Honorary Vice-President of the Santa Fe Disneyland Railroad. Needless to say, my siblings were less than pleased, especially Grant and Harry, who I had let go before me in line. Soon, Walt had joined us, along with Engineer Bill, while the Disneyland Band added some lively Disney music to help mark this special occasion.

There were about half a dozen photographers there, and they had us pose for some photos, both in the cab of the Ernest S. Marsh and with the boxcar filled with bright and shiny pennies. After that, I got to ride in the cab and 'drive' the train around the park, which was a highlight of the entire ceremony. We went around Disneyland only once, stopping at all the stops.

Raymond, Walt, and Engineer Bill,
a local TV personality, pose aboard the Ernest S. Marsh

Afterwards, a young woman took us on a tour of the park. We rode all the rides we wanted to ride, and I don't remember having to wait in any lines. Later in the day, while riding in the wheelhouse of the Mark Twain Riverboat, mom suggested that I let Harry pilot the boat, since he had been whining that he should have been the winner that day.

After Raymond's big day, his family continued on to Maryland. The boxcar and pennies would arrive soon afterward, having been shipped from Disneyland.

Disneyland fans will want to know... "So, whatever happened to the boxcar and 10,000 pennies?" Raymond opened his very first bank account with all of the pennies once he arrived in Maryland, and the boxcar was ultimately stored in the garage of the family home, along with the Revell HO scale Santa Fe Electric Train Set he had also received from Walt that day. Unfortunately, a house fire in the fall of 1970 consumed both the boxcar and the train set, leaving nothing of either, only memories of a very special day for a lucky 8 year-old boy at Disneyland.

Raymond opens his first bank account with his 10,000 pennies, accompanied by his unique Disneyland boxcar

A PARTING STORY

As you finish *Disney History - Rare & Unknown*, I'd like to leave you with a fun and amusing story that was shared with me by John Kuri...

After the park's opening Dad and Walt would meet every Wednesday for a walk through with a few other key executives and designers. It was usually a group of five: Walt, Dad, a Park executive, (Joe Fowler, later it would be Dick Nunis) Dick Irvine from WED (now known as Imagineering) plus another designated WED representative. On one of those days as the group was exiting Tomorrowland towards the Main Street Hub, the Plaza Inn patio had quite a few tables littered with dirty dishes and unoccupied. No busboys were in evidence. Walt walked into the patio, went directly to the gate that opened to the "Backlot" area where there was access to the kitchen. He saw three busboys taking a smoke break. Walt said, "Hey fellows, there's a lot of dirty dishes out there. Why don't you stagger your breaks so our guests have clean tables?" One of them piped up and dismissively said...

"Who do you think you are, Walt Disney?"

The Operations person from the Park intervened and the busboy's break ended. Meanwhile, Walt turned and went back into the patio, turned to the group and said, "I want a conveyor belt designed and installed in all our patios so that dishes can be sent directly to the kitchen wash area."

About the Author

Disney historian and author Mike Westby is a former third-party product developer for six different divisions of the Walt Disney Company, including Disney Cruise Line, Epcot Marketing, Walt Disney World Resort, and Disneyland Resort Merchandizing. In addition, he has developed more than a dozen different iPhone and Android apps for the Disney theme parks, as well as authored four books relating to the work of the Disney Imagineers and Disney history. As part of the product development for these various projects, he spent many, many hours scouring and photographing the Disney parks prior to them opening to guests, and it was during these photo shoots that he began to take note of and appreciate the countless small details and props that the Disney Imagineers had purposely placed or hidden throughout the parks, with many containing an intricate and puzzling reference to an obscure story element tied directly to the history of the company, be it a reflection of Walt Disney himself, Mickey Mouse, different Disney Legends, artists, and Imagineers, or even the creation of Disneyland and Walt Disney World Resort. As a result, Mike developed an interest in the history of Walt Disney and his theme parks, as well as a talent for conducting extensive research into the undiscovered and untold back stories of obscure moments in the rich and varied story that is Disney history. Through this, he has discovered and shared with readers many untold stories and rare artifacts that have never before been published in any Disney-related books, articles, or web sites, including the publication of a nearly 100 year-old never-before-seen and possibly one-of-a-kind business card belonging to Walt Disney from his days at the Walt Disney Studios on Hyperion Avenue, his discovery of Ub Iwerks' actual childhood home in Kansas City, the first ever published photo and backstory of George Lloyd, the man who hand-carved the elaborate "Capitol of Disneyland", the first-ever published *complete* story behind the creation of the very first Hidden Mickey, the never-before-seen ad placed by Ub Iwerks for his Iwwerks Art Service business, which changes the narrative of Walt and Ub's time after their Iwwerks-Disney Commercial Artists business folded in Kansas City, the untold story of whatever happened to the special Disneyland Railroad boxcar filled with 10,000 pennies that Walt awarded 8 year-old Raymond Sleeper in August of 1960, and many others.

Today, you'll find Mike visiting the parks and other Disney-related sites, poring over periodicals, newspapers, articles, and books from the 1920s through 1940s, buying a rare Disney artifact just for its information, sifting through Kansas City tax records, studying hundreds of old photos for minute details, and of course interviewing Disney Legends, Disney Imagineers, and other Disney notables to uncover another untold Disney story to share with his fellow Disney history enthusiasts.

ACKNOWLEDGMENTS

Many people have graciously contributed to the development of this book. From Marty Sklar's information about the early days of *The Disneyland News* to Bob Gurr's stories and generous comments, as well as help with details, photos, information, and stories from generous Disney Imagineers and other Disney notables. Thank you for helping me write a title that contains not only quality content, but also family value entertainment which is respectful of the legacy of Walt Disney.

For that, I would like to thank you all...

- Bob Gurr - Disney Legend and Imagineer
- Brian Hillman - George H. Lloyd Relative
- Brian & Meghan Westby - Disney Researchers
- Conrad Naydiuk - Disney Researcher
- Cindy Bothner - Walt Disney Imagineering
- Dave Drumheller - WDWGuidedTours.com
- David Lesjak - Disney Historian and Author
- Elijah Winkler - Kansas City Public Library
- Frank Reifsnyder - Walt Disney Imagineering
- George Eldridge - Decoding the Disneyland Telegraph
- Glenn Barker - Walt Disney Imagineering
- John A. Kuri - Disney Legend Emile Kuri's son
- Jordan Sallis - George H. Lloyd Relative
- Kristy Westby - Research Technician
- Marty Sklar - Principal Creative Executive for The Walt Disney Company
- Megan Westby - Disneyland Photographer
- Michael & Sharon Broggie - Disney Historians and Authors
- Michael Campbell - President Emeritus, Carolwood Pacific Historical Society
- Ray Kinman - Disney Imagineer
- Scott Cauger - Grandson of A.V. Cauger
- Steve DeGaetano - Disneyland Railroad Historian - SteamPassages.com
- Terry Peterson - Disney Imagineer
- The Disney Archives

And most of all my parents, Richard & Roberta, for taking me to Disneyland for the very first time many years ago!

Additional Books by Mike Westby

"Almost every page contained details I had never noticed before."

- Disney Legend Bob Gurr

If you enjoyed reading *Disney History - Rare & Unknown*, then you're sure to enjoy *The Hidden Secrets & Stories of Disneyland*, written under the pen name of Mike Fox. Similar in scope to this title, it is a fun and entertaining look at **over 250** of the magical secrets and story elements hidden throughout Disneyland by the Disney Imagineers...all arranged as a fun tour and complete with **more than 220** photos!

Available Online at the Walt Disney Family Museum, the Walt Disney Hometown Museum, and Elsewhere

THE HIDDEN SECRETS & STORIES OF WALT DISNEY WORLD

"A true treasure trove of new information."

- **Didier Ghez** - Author of Disneyland Paris - From Sketch to Reality

The Hidden Secrets & Stories of Walt Disney World is an entertaining and magical in-depth look at the secret details and story elements the Disney Imagineers have purposely hidden throughout Walt Disney World for guests to discover and enjoy...all arranged as a fun tour and complete with photos!

Through countless park visits, interviews, and untold hours of in-depth research, *The Hidden Secrets & Stories of Walt Disney World* presents **over 500** fun, whimsical, and fascinating details, including never-before-published stories and photos.

Would You Like to Share or Sell a Rare Piece of Disney History?

If you own a rare or never-before-seen piece of Disney history, be it an early Disney merchandise item, an item from Walt's days in Marceline or Kansas City, a piece from the early days of Disneyland, a rare document, a note written by Walt, or most any rare or old Disney item, I'd love to hear about it! Feel free to send me an email and we can talk Disney. And if you're interested in selling an item, we can talk about that, too. It may or may not be something I'm looking to add to my collection, but I'd love to see it, as it may be the perfect piece to kick off some in-depth research for another article in this book! You can reach me at Mike.Westby@Comcast.net.

Disney History - Rare & Unknown

Selected Bibliography

Many different sources of content, including interviews, books, articles, documents, vintage publications, correspondence, photos, video and theme park visits were used in the research for this book.

The following are some of the publications which were not only helpful, but I would highly recommend them as reading material for anyone interested in Disney history.

Broggie, Michael. *Walt Disney's Railroad Story.* Donning Company Publishers, 4th Edition. 2014

Burnes, Brian - Butler, Robert W. - Viets, Dan. *Walt Disney's Missouri - The Roots of a Creative Genius.* 2002

Canemaker, John. *Winsor McCay - His Life and Art.* 2005

DeGaetano, Steve. *The Disneyland Railroad - A Complete History in Words and Pictures.* Collector's Edition

Gabler, Neal. *Walt Disney: The Triumph of the American Imagination.* Alfred A. Knopf, 2006

Groskopf, Jeremy. The American Silent Cinema - Profit and the Margins. Indiana University Press. 2021

Iwerks, Don. *Walt Disney's Ultimate Inventor - The Genius of Ub Iwerks.* Disney Editions, 2019

Lesjak, David. *In The Service Of The Red Cross - Walt Disney's Early Adventures - 1918 - 1919*

Lloyd, George. *George H. Lloyd's Hand Carved Caenstone Model of Our National Capitol.* Lowenstein's, Approx. 1943

Sklar, Marty. *Dream It! Do It!: My Half-Century Creating Disney's Magic Kingdoms.* Disney Editions, 2013

Smith, Dave. *Disney A to Z: The Updated Official Encyclopedia.* Disney Editions, 1998

Strodder, Chris. *The Disneyland Encyclopedia.* Santa Monica Press, 2012

Thomas, Bob. *Walt Disney: An American Original.* Hyperion, 1994

Walt Disney Hometown Museum - *Guided Tour of Marceline, Missouri.*

In addition:

- American Legion Post 264 - Marceline, MO
- Bentonian Yearbook - 1925, 1926, and 1931 Editions
- Billy Ireland Cartoon Library & Museum - Ohio State University
- D23.com
- Disney.com
- Downtown Marceline Foundation
- Illustrating Edwin - A Bio of Edwin G. Lutz - EGLutz.com
- Kansas City Census - 1910
- Kansas City Historic Preservation Office
- Kansas City Pubic Library - KCLibrary.org
    - Special thanks to Elijah Winkler
- Kansas City Star Newspapers - 1907 - 1918
- Missouri Valley Special Collections - KC Public Library
- Thank You Walt Disney, Inc.
- The Kansas Citian - University of Illinois
- The National Archives
- The Walt Disney Boyhood Home
- The Walt Disney Family Museum
- The Walt Disney Hometown Museum
- www.MechanicalMusicPress.com

DESCHUTES RIVER
PRESS

Made in the USA
Coppell, TX
11 February 2026

71789386R00144